CONTENTS

Scales and sizes
The *Cars in space* section of this book contains scale drawings of space rovers against a human body to show their size.

6 ft (1.8 m)

1931 La Salle

What is a car?

A car is a vehicle that is specifically designed to carry people. Its basic structure is made up of a steel frame called a chassis. A typical car has four wheels and is powered by an engine, which uses fuel of some kind.

Steering wheel moves the wheels to change the car's direction

Wiper cleans dirt off the windshield and gives the driver a clear view of the road ahead

Dashboard features controls and instruments, such as the speedometer and the fuel gauge

Hood covers the engine

Battery powers electrical systems, such as lights and ignition

Grille allows air into the radiator, helping to keep the engine cool

Engine powers the car's movement

On the inside

All the functions of a car are controlled from the interior with the help of a steering wheel, gear stick, and foot pedals. The seats are padded for comfort.

Headlight lights the road at night

Fender stops spray and grit flying from off the tires

Antenna receives signals
for the in-car radio

Trunk can be used
to store luggage

Window pillar gives
strength to the car's frame

Window allows nearly
all-around vision from interior

Rear light indicates
when the car is braking

Bumper acts as a
cushion against impacts

Axle (metal
bar) connects
the wheels

Wheel turns on an axle

Door gives the driver
and any passengers
access to interior

Door mirror lets the
driver see rear and side

HOT AND COLD

Numerous tests are carried out on a new
car model to make sure that all parts perform
as expected in extreme weather conditions.
This car is being tested to check if all its
parts work efficiently in freezing conditions.

History of the car

Cars have come a long way since the first self-propelled vehicle hit the road in 1769. Over the years, numerous inventions and technological developments have helped to shape the cars that we drive today.

Otto cycle engine

1769: Nicolas Cugnot of France invents a steam-powered cart, with a top speed of 2.5 mph (4 kph).

1876: Nikolaus August Otto of Germany creates an internal combustion four-stroke engine.

1750–1850	1860	1870	1880

1885: Karl Benz designs and builds the world's first gas vehicle, powered by an internal combustion engine.

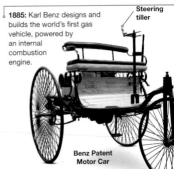

Steering tiller

Benz Patent Motor Car

1865: The UK's new "Locomotives on Highways Act" states that all mechanized vehicles must have three drivers, go no faster than 4 mph (6.5 kph) on the road, and follow a man walking ahead, waving a red warning flag.

Motorized carriage

1886: Gottlieb Daimler of Germany fits a gas engine to a horseless carriage, creating the world's first four-wheeled gas car. It reaches 10 mph (16 kph).

1890　　　　　　1900

1889: In France, René Panhard and Émile Levassor become the world's first car manufacturers, building motor vehicles for sale.

1891: René Panhard builds the first car with an engine at the front.

Panhard's Phaeton

GAME CHANGERS

Certain cars changed the history of the car industry. Hugely popular in their day, these cars are now prized classics.

BENZ VELO
Before 1894, each new car was unique. The first car built to a standard design was the Benz Velo—134 identical Velos were produced.

MERCEDES-BENZ 260D
The first diesel passenger car—the Mercedes-Benz 260D—arrived in 1936. By 1939, there was a 15-month waiting list for the car.

THE BEETLE
Volkswagen started the mass-market production of the Type 38 (later called the Beetle) in Germany, in 1938.

FERRARI 125 SPORT
In 1947, the Ferrari 125 Sport was launched—the first car under the Ferrari brand name.

THE AUSTIN MINI
An affordable small car, the Austin Mini had a spacious interior. It was launched as an alternative to the slow and unsafe microcars (very small cars) of the 1950s.

1923: Alfred Sloan, president of General Motors, introduces the idea of changing a car's style every year.

1900: Wilhelm Maybach creates the Mercedes 35 hp race car, with a top speed of 53 mph (86 kph).

1900	1910	1920	1930	1940	1950

1901: The two-seater Oldsmobile Curved Dash arrives. It is the USA's first mass-produced gas-powered car, with 425 cars built in its first year.

1908: The iconic Ford Model T is launched. It is the first low-priced mass-produced car, built using inexpensive raw materials.

2008: India's Tata Motors launches Nano—a rear-engined, gas-driven car. It was advertised as the world's cheapest new car.

1964: The Pontiac GTO, regarded as the first "muscle car," is produced, launching an era of "muscle cars" in the USA.

Pontiac GTO

1997: Toyota unveils the Prius—the world's first commercially mass-produced and marketed hybrid car—in Japan.

| 1960 | 1970 | 1980 | 1990 | 2000 | 2010 | 2020 |

1972: Victor Wouk builds the first full-powered, full-size hybrid test vehicle, based on a 1972 Buick Skylark from General Motors.

1981: The Mercedes-Benz W 126-series S-Class sedan becomes the first car with a driver airbag fitted as standard.

2008: BYD, a former Chinese battery manufacturer, launches the F3DM—the world's first mass-produced plug-in hybrid sedan car.

F3DM

How an engine works

Most cars today are powered by an internal combustion engine. This is so-called because inside ("internal") the engine, small explosions ("combustion") make pistons move. This moves other parts to turn the car's wheels.

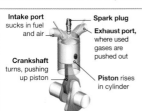

Intake port sucks in fuel and air

Spark plug

Exhaust port, where used gases are pushed out

Crankshaft turns, pushing up piston

Piston rises in cylinder

Engine cylinders

Internal combustion engines contain cylinders. When the engine fires, a rod called the crankshaft pushes a piston up into each cylinder, squeezing a fuel-air mixture. A tiny explosion results, pushing the piston down again. This is repeated along all the cylinders, keeping the crankshaft turning.

From engine to wheels

The crankshaft collects power from the cylinders and transfers it to the wheels via the gearbox. In a front-wheel drive car, as shown here, the gears inside the gearbox turn to pass on the power to two places—the front axle, which controls the front wheels, and the drive shaft, which works the rear axle and the rear wheels.

TYPES OF ENGINE

Internal combustion engine designs vary in the number of cylinders they have, and how they are arranged.

In a **flat-four**, two cylinders are placed horizontally on each side of the crankshaft, providing extra balance.

A **straight-four**, or inline, is the most common layout. It has an upright, or slanting, row of four cylinders and makes efficient use of fuel.

In a **V6 engine**, two rows of three cylinders are arranged in a "V." It is good for high-performance and racing cars.

Front and rear axles (rodlike parts) transmit power to the wheels

In **front-wheel drive** (where only the front wheels are powered), the engine is always in the front

Gears alter the engine's power so the wheels turn at the speed the driver needs

The **drive shaft** carries power to the rear wheels

Inside a factory

Car production is a complex process. Cars are built on an assembly line, where the procedure is split into many stages, involving robots as well as humans. Several quality checks and tests are carried out before the cars are finally transported to the showroom.

Freshly painted

After the car's body is put together, it is prepared for painting. Robots spray several layers of paint onto it. After the final coat, the car is placed on a conveyer that takes it to be "baked" at high temperatures, which makes the paint more durable.

Making the car body

Metal sheets (usually steel or aluminum) are cut and molded to form the body panels and roof of each car. These are welded onto the car's frame by robots. Each car is then given its own vehicle identification number (VIN).

Finishing the job

After being painted, cars are moved along the assembly line to be fitted with parts. The engine and gearbox are pushed into place from underneath. Robots then fix the doors and wheels to the chassis. At this stage, all other components of the car, such as the steering wheel and electrical systems, are fixed to their respective places.

Ready to go

The cars then go through various tests to check that all the different components—such as the brakes, engine, and steering wheel—are functioning properly. Finally, each car is cleared to be sent to the showroom.

New car, old car

Around 60 million cars are produced each year. After leaving the factory, the cars are transported to showrooms where they are put on sale, or exported for sale in other countries. A car owner may resell his vehicle, or send it to a scrapyard if it is beyond repair. At the scrapyard, different parts of the car are recycled to be used again.

Cars can be driven on and off a **car carrier**

Leaving the factory

New cars are delivered locally by train or in car transporters. They are also exported on ships called car carriers. A large car carrier can hold 8,000 cars. The biggest car carrier, the *Triple-E*, can carry 36,000 cars!

Each car has a **protective cover** while being transported

RECYCLING

Most countries have recycling laws. About 80 percent of a car can be recycled.

Goodbye, car!

Few cars end up in landfill. Most go to a scrapyard to be stripped for spare parts that can be used to repair other cars. Fluids, such as oil and antifreeze, are sent for recycling, along with the tires and metal body parts.

A car's engine may be reconditioned (restored) or the metal may be recycled.

Crush that car!

The remains of old or smashed cars are often squashed. They are then easier to transport to a recycling plant for melting down.

Crushed cars

The chassis (base) of a car is usually melted down for the metal it contains.

The **heavy metals** and chemicals in car batteries can also be reused.

Safety measures

New cars undergo a lot of tests to make sure they are safe to drive. One of the most valuable of these tests is the use of crash test dummies—life-sized models of people. The results from these tests are recorded and analyzed to improve a car's design as well as safety features, such as airbags and seat belts.

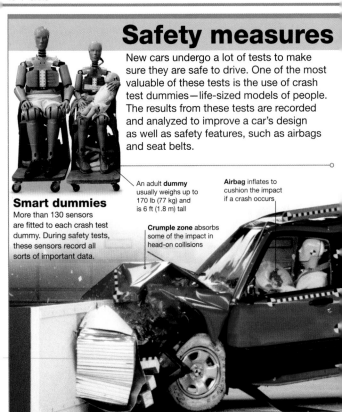

Smart dummies

More than 130 sensors are fitted to each crash test dummy. During safety tests, these sensors record all sorts of important data.

An adult **dummy** usually weighs up to 170 lb (77 kg) and is 6 ft (1.8 m) tall

Airbag inflates to cushion the impact if a crash occurs

Crumple zone absorbs some of the impact in head-on collisions

Track testing

Various track tests study how a new car will perform on the road. For example, a "moose" test studies how well a car can swerve to avoid obstacles that may suddenly appear.

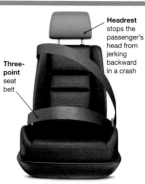

Headrest stops the passenger's head from jerking backward in a crash

Three-point seat belt

Safety belt

Seat belts ensure that a car's passengers do not fall out of their seats in the event of a crash. It is the law to wear a seat belt in most countries.

What if it crashes?

Modern cars are built to absorb the impact of a crash. For this, each end of the car has a crumple zone—an area designed to crush and crumple on collision. Airbags are additional safety features, which quickly inflate to cushion the front seat occupants in the event of a crash.

Tire needs good tread (grip) and correct air pressure to steer and brake efficiently

Engineers use mist or
smoke illuminated by

lasers

to study the way air flows around
a car in a wind tunnel

WIND TUNNEL TESTING
A wind tunnel is a huge, tubelike structure with huge electric fans at one end that create high speed winds. A car undergoing the test is parked inside this tunnel. Different instruments help to study the airflow around the car and test how aerodynamic it is. Cutting through the air accounts for around 15 percent of a car's fuel use, so wind tunnel testing is important to a car's designers.

Early cars

The earliest cars were steam-powered. They were usually simple carriages equipped with an engine, because car makers were heavily influenced by the design of horse-drawn carriages. Inventors then tried to build cars suitable for everyday use, which led to the appearance of engines powered by gas and electricity. Many other innovations, such as the windshield wiper and steering wheel, followed.

FUEL METER
In 1914, car manufacturer Studebaker installed the first dash-mounted gas gauge, showing how much fuel was in the car. These became a standard feature in the 1920s.

Cars from the past

Early powered vehicles were "horseless carts" driven by steam, and the first designs were inspired by carriages. The late 19th century saw several technological developments, but the age of cars truly began in 1908 with Henry Ford's moving assembly line for his Model T.

Making way for motors

The first working self-propelled, mechanical vehicle was built in France in 1769 by Nicolas Cugnot (1725–1804). It was steam-powered and could carry four people, but was slow and unstable.

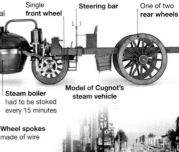

Single front wheel

Steering bar

One of two **rear wheels**

Steam boiler had to be stoked every 15 minutes

Model of Cugnot's steam vehicle

Wheel spokes made of wire

Shaping up

In 1889, Gottlieb Daimler unveiled his gas-powered car—the first vehicle to be designed specifically as a car. Until then, carriages were equipped with engines to be used as cars.

Model T

Henry Ford's moving assembly line revolutionized car manufacturing by making the mass production of vehicles faster and more organized. The Ford Motor Company sold more than 15 million Model T cars between 1908 and 1927.

Changing face

The 1920s were a golden age for the car industry as cars became smaller and more affordable and reliable, attracting more buyers. Sports cars, such as this 1927 OM 665 Superba, were also developed for leisure use and racing.

After the war

By the 1950s, the market for cars had grown as companies began to sell their models to international markets as well. Many American families owned a car and the roads became busier.

Before 1920

Building the first cars was a remarkable feat. However, manufacturing them in large numbers and convincing the public to buy these new types of vehicle proved to be hard. Until about 1920, the US was producing the most cars, followed by France, the UK, and Germany.

Peugeot Type 5

The Type 5 was the second gas car model that Peugeot came out with after the Type 2. It had face-to-face seating. In 1894, this car took part in the world's first motor car competition.

YEAR	1894
ORIGIN	France
ENGINE	565 cc, twin-cylinder
TOP SPEED	11 mph (18 kph)

Arrol-Johnston 10 HP Dogcart

Developed by George Johnston in Glasgow, Scotland, the Dogcart was the first car to be built in the UK, remaining in production for a decade. The model was designed with its engine placed below the floor of the car.

YEAR	1897
ORIGIN	UK
ENGINE	3,230 cc, flat-two
TOP SPEED	25 mph (40 kph)

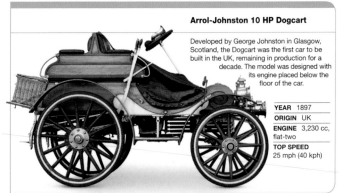

Mercedes 60 hp

One of the most advanced cars of its time in terms of engineering and design, the Mercedes 60 hp was among the fastest cars in the early 1900s. Its design was aimed at improving passenger comfort.

YEAR	1903
ORIGIN	Germany
ENGINE	9,236 cc, straight-four
TOP SPEED	73 mph (117 kph)

Hood

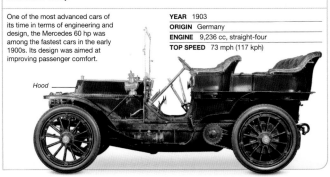

Rolls-Royce Silver Ghost 40/50 hp

At first, only one car in the 40/50 hp series was called Silver Ghost. Later, all cars of this model were given this name. It became known as a reliable car and was produced until 1925.

YEAR	1906
ORIGIN	UK
ENGINE	7,036 cc, straight-six
TOP SPEED	75 mph (121 kph)

1920–1935

As affordable car models became available in the 1920s, the demand for cars gradually grew. Sports and race cars also gained popularity. By the 1930s, smaller, more aerodynamic, and more technologically advanced cars were being produced.

FOCUS ON...
SERVICES

The increase in the sale of cars led to growth in other businesses, such as gas stations, repair shops, and motels.

▲ Before the first gas station was built in 1905 in Missouri gas was sold at pharmacies.

▲ As long-distance travel became common, motor hotels—or motels—began to appear along major American roads, providing cheap accommodation for travelers.

▲ Other roadside businesses, such as diners and similar places to eat, also thrived.

Bugatti Type 35B

The Type 35 was a successful race car and could also be driven on roads. A member of the Type 35 family, the Type 35B was the last version to be produced in the series.

YEAR	1927
ORIGIN	France
ENGINE	2,262 cc, straight-eight
TOP SPEED	127 mph (204 kph)

Mudguard for use on road

Small windshield to shield driver from wind

Eight-spoke, cast-aluminum wheel

Duesenberg Model J

The fastest and most powerful car in the American market at the time it was produced, the Model J was designed to appeal to the rich and famous. It was also launched in Europe, where it proved a worthy competitor to the big, luxurious cars already available there.

YEAR	1928
ORIGIN	USA
ENGINE	6,882 cc, straight-eight
TOP SPEED	119 mph (192 kph)

Ford Model Y

Made in the UK for markets outside the US, the Ford Model Y was seen as Ford's first "foreign" car. It sold well enough to give Ford the leading position among car manufacturers.

YEAR	1932
ORIGIN	UK
ENGINE	933 cc, straight-four
TOP SPEED	57 mph (92 kph)

This step is called a running board

Only 14

**egg-shaped, three-wheeler
Brütsch Mopettas
were ever built**

MICROCAR
Designed in 1956, the Brütsch Mopetta was the smallest of a number of microcars (very small cars) built by Egon Brütsch. It measured 67 in (1.7 m) long and 35 in (0.9 m) wide and was powered by a 50-cc engine. With a body made completely from fiberglass, it weighed just 172 lb (78 kg).

The 1940s and 1950s

During World War II (1939–45), cars were largely produced for military purposes. After the war, affordable and simple family cars were in demand. By the 1950s, however, there was a call for glamour, performance, and style.

Willys MB Jeep

Made for the military, this Jeep was a light, four-wheel drive (where the engine powers all four wheels) utility vehicle for cargo transport and surveillance. It is an iconic World War II car.

YEAR	1941
ORIGIN	USA
ENGINE	2,199 cc, straight-four
TOP SPEED	60 mph (97 kph)

Dodge Coronet

The Dodge Coronet was available in a four-door and a two-door model. This car's clutch was replaced by a fluid-drive transmission, which was operated by a foot pedal. This meant that the driver could stop the car and then start it again in any gear, without using the gear stick or clutch.

YEAR	1949
ORIGIN	USA
ENGINE	3,769 cc, straight-six
TOP SPEED	80 mph (129 kph)

"Whitewall" tires have a ring of white rubber

Chevrolet Bel Air

Compared to the first Bel Air 1950 model, the 1955 Chevrolet Bel Air boasted a more stylish design, attractive chrome features, and a better engine. The combination made it one of the most desirable cars of its time, and it continues to be prized by collectors.

YEAR	1955
ORIGIN	USA
ENGINE	4,343 cc, V8
TOP SPEED	100 mph (161 kph)

Two-tone paintwork highlights car's sleek appearance

Hooded headlight was a new style feature on this model

Renault Dauphine

After conducting a survey of European drivers in 1951, Renault improved its 4CV economy car and launched the hugely successful Dauphine. This car had a larger engine and more spacious interior than the 4CV. It recorded worldwide sales of two million cars in 12 years.

YEAR	1956
ORIGIN	France
ENGINE	845 cc, straight-four
TOP SPEED	66 mph (106 kph)

The 1960s and 1970s

In the 1960s, cars with simple, almost boxlike, designs became popular. Cars were more compact or more luxurious, while also increasing in their performance and power. In the 1970s, efficiency improved further and safety measures, such as seat belts and airbags, were introduced.

Mini Cooper

The Mini was a small, energy-efficient car that was launched in 1959. In 1961, Formula 1 car designer John Cooper improved its design—adding disk brakes, a powerful motor, and wider wheels—and created the Mini Cooper.

YEAR 1961

ORIGIN UK

ENGINE 1,275 cc, four-cylinder

TOP SPEED 100 mph (161 kph)

Although only 10 ft (3 m) long, the Mini had enough room inside for a whole family

Jaguar XJ6

Perhaps one of the most significant cars in the company's history, the XJ6 replaced most of Jaguar's sedans. Its design was said to offer a perfect balance of comfort, performance, and power.

YEAR	1968
ORIGIN	UK
ENGINE	4,235 cc, six-cylinder
TOP SPEED	124 mph (200 kph)

Citroën SM

In 1968, Citroën purchased the Italian luxury car manufacturer Maserati. Their collaboration resulted in the Citroën SM in 1970. This car combined Citroën's aerodynamic design with Maserati's powerful V6 engine.

YEAR	1970
ORIGIN	France
ENGINE	2,670 cc, V6
TOP SPEED	142 mph (229 kph)

Modern cars

From the 1980s, cars were increasingly equipped with new technology, such as parking assistance. Existing features, including the steering wheel and dashboard, were improved. Today, cars are often built with extra features, such as navigation systems and rearview cameras. Engines are more powerful and fuel efficient than in the past and can handle longer distances.

OFF-ROADING
Sport utility vehicles (SUVs) are designed for "off-roading," where cars are driven on rough terrains, such as in and around forests and over sand.

All shapes and sizes

A buyer chooses a car for its features, depending on individual requirements. A family may need more seats, a larger trunk, and four or even five doors, as opposed to two. Some people may opt for additional features, such as a sunroof.

Door design

Most car doors are hinged and can be opened manually or, in heavier models, electronically. Some cars have child-safety locks on their rear doors, so that passengers, especially children, do not accidentally open the doors from inside.

The hatchback is a fifth door and opens upward

Roof design

Most cars have a solid roof. They may be fitted with a sunroof (sliding pane). Convertible cars have a retractable roof that folds away or a detachable roof that is taken off.

Trunk space

The trunk space of an station wagon is designed for carrying bulky loads, but even small cars have enough space for carrying shopping bags and luggage.

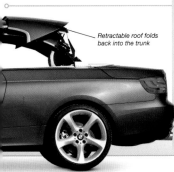

Retractable roof folds back into the trunk

BOX DESIGN

The **box design** of a car shows how the car's three main areas—its engine, passenger space, and trunk space—are divided into diff--erent sections.

In a **one-box** design, the whole interior of the car—including the engine and trunk—is designed as one compartment.

A **two-box** design is one in which the engine forms a separate compartment from the passenger and trunk space.

A **three-box** design divides the car into three sections—the engine, passenger space, and trunk space.

FOCUS ON...
REAR DESIGN

Sedans are grouped according to the shape and slope of the rear section of the car.

▲ In a fastback, the slope stretches from the roof to the base of the trunk.

▲ In a notchback sedan, the trunk lid and the roof are parallel to the ground. The lid extends back horizontally from the rear windshield.

▲ In a hatchback, the trunk lid covers the entire rear. The rear windshield lifts up with the lid.

Sedans

Sedan cars have a fixed roof and an enclosed trunk, and most models have four doors. Types of sedan include large family cars, compacts with a smaller rear space, luxury models with powerful engines, and high-performing sports sedans.

Maserati Biturbo

The Maserati brand, known for its high-priced models, wanted to introduce a supercar-style vehicle that was more affordable. The result was the two-door Maserati Biturbo. The car sold well at first, mainly because of its luxurious interior. However, because of technical problems, including engine failures and oil leaks, sales dropped.

YEAR	1981
ORIGIN	Italy
ENGINE	1,996 cc, V6
TOP SPEED	132 mph (212 kph)

The 1984 version of the Maserati Biturbo, with a modified engine, was named the Worst Car of 1984 by *Time* magazine in 2007.

Chrysler LHS

Chrysler's first true sports sedan (a car that combines the design of a sports car with the luxury of a sedan), the Chrysler LHS is known for its aerodynamic shape, which greatly reduces wind noise inside the car. Its luxury features and good engine performance add to its appeal.

YEAR	1994
ORIGIN	USA
ENGINE	3,518 cc, V6
TOP SPEED	136 mph (219 kph)

Bentley Arnage

The sporty, high-end Bentley Arnage was the first car for Bentley Motors to have a completely new design since 1980. Equipped with a special V8 engine, it was a fast and elegant car. The last Bentley Arnage was produced in 2009.

YEAR	1998
ORIGIN	UK
ENGINE	4,398 cc, V8
TOP SPEED	150 mph (241 kph)

Volvo S60

This Volvo was designed to compete with German-made sedans. A number of speed-record attempts and track racing events have shown how powerful the car is. The S60 is even used as a patrol car by some police forces.

YEAR 2000

ORIGIN Sweden

ENGINE 2,484 cc, straight-five

TOP SPEED 130 mph (210 kph)

Toyota Camry

The Toyota Camry has been one of the best-selling sedans in the US since 1997. The redesigned model has more room inside, although a smaller trunk space, than earlier versions of the car.

YEAR 2007

ORIGIN Japan

ENGINE 2,362 cc, straight-four

TOP SPEED 130 mph (210 kph)

Toyota has a tradition of using the word "crown" in the names of most of its cars. "Camry" comes from a Japanese word for crown.

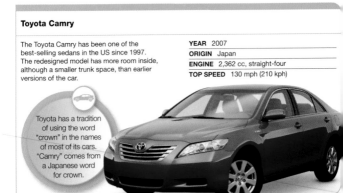

BMW 335i

The 335i is extremely powerful. It is the first car in BMW's 3 Series to have a turbocharged gas engine (extra-powerful yet compact). However, like all German cars, its top speed is artificially limited to 155 mph (250 kph)—high enough for driving on the autobahn (highways that do not have a speed limit).

YEAR	2007
ORIGIN	Germany
ENGINE	2,979 cc, straight-six
TOP SPEED	155 mph (250 kph)

Headlights swivel in the same direction as the steering wheel

Jaguar XJ

Although the Jaguar XJ is a full-sized sedan, its aluminum body makes it lighter than even a standard medium-sized car. Its glass roof extends over the rear seats.

YEAR	2010
ORIGIN	UK
ENGINE	5,000 cc, V8
TOP SPEED	155 mph (250 kph)

Sensors on the windshield automatically activate windshield wipers when it rains

Toyota Corolla Altis

Toyota made the first Corolla in 1966. The 2011 model is the 12th variation. Like all the Corollas in the past, the Altis' design is focused on reliability over style and technology, though the new engine is smoother and more fuel-efficient.

YEAR 2011

ORIGIN Japan

ENGINE 1,987 cc, straight-four

TOP SPEED 115 mph (185 kph)

Audi A3

The demand for Audi cars in China was one of the factors that led the company to design a sedan version of the A3 series. It has a high-performance engine and a luxury design, but less luggage space than the hatchback version.

YEAR 2013

ORIGIN Germany

ENGINE 1,781 cc, straight-four

TOP SPEED 151 mph (243 kph)

Honda Amaze

The midsized Honda Amaze is the sedan version of the hatchback Honda Brio. Although the Amaze shares the same engine as the Brio, its color options and overall layout, it is set apart by a much larger trunk.

YEAR 2013

ORIGIN Japan

ENGINE 1,198 cc, straight-four

TOP SPEED 87 mph (140 kph)

Mercedes-Benz C220 CDI AMG Sport Edition

The C-Class is the second-smallest sedan produced by Mercedes. The AMG Sport Edition has a range of performance features from AMG, the in-house racing engine division of Mercedes-Benz.

YEAR	2014
ORIGIN	Germany
ENGINE	2,143 cc, straight-four
TOP SPEED	144 mph (232 kph)

Hatchbacks

A hatchback gets its name from the sloping door at the back of the car's body—called a hatch—that opens upward. This door is hinged at the top, and it covers a trunk, or luggage space, at the rear. Because they are smaller than sedans, hatchbacks are easier to park, which makes them a popular choice for people living in cities.

Fiat Uno

Among small family cars (superminis), the Fiat Uno stands out for its modern seating design, with slightly elevated seats, earning it the nickname "the ultimate supermini." Its aerodynamic design, spacious interior, and fuel efficiency earned it the European Car of the Year award in 1984.

YEAR	1983
ORIGIN	Italy
ENGINE	1,301 cc, straight-four
TOP SPEED	104 mph (167 kph)

The Fiat Uno is the most-produced Fiat car: more than 8,800,000 cars have been built over eight years.

Peugeot 205 GTi

With this model, Peugeot became one of the first brands to create a successful sporty hatchback. Its features include alloy wheels, additional driving lights, and larger bumpers.

YEAR	1984
ORIGIN	France
ENGINE	1,905 cc, straight-four
TOP SPEED	121 mph (195 kph)

Volkswagen New Beetle

This car was inspired by the original "bug-shaped" Volkswagen Beetle. The New Beetle shares many similar features with its ancestor, such as large round rear lights and a rounded roof.

YEAR	1998
ORIGIN	Germany
ENGINE	1,984 cc, straight-four
TOP SPEED	115 mph (185 kph)

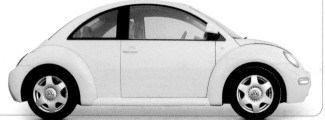

Maruti Suzuki Swift

The Japanese Suzuki Swift was sold in various
markets worldwide before being launched in
India as the Maruti Suzuki Swift. Its European-style
curvy body and sporty performance made it a
popular choice among hatchbacks.

Stretched rear light

YEAR 2005

ORIGIN India

ENGINE 1,197 cc,
straight-four

TOP SPEED
100 mph
(160 kph)

Peugeot 107

This car's small size makes it ideal
for city driving, and its carbon dioxide
emissions are much lower than most
other hatchbacks. However, it has
limited trunk space and lacks
advanced safety systems.

YEAR 2005

ORIGIN France

ENGINE 998 cc,
straight-three

TOP SPEED
98 mph
(158 kph)

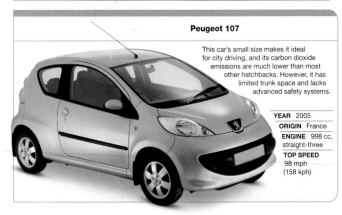

Honda Fit Sport

Unlike the earlier Honda Fit models, the Sport has four different seat options. This allows owners to increase trunk or seating space based on their requirements.

YEAR 2007

ORIGIN Japan

ENGINE 1,497 cc, straight-four

TOP SPEED 114 mph (183 kph)

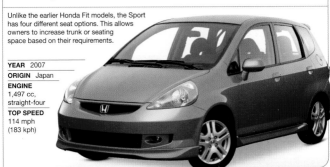

Tata Nano

The world's cheapest new car, the Tata Nano is manufactured by Tata Motors in India. Its design includes cost-saving features. For example, its engine is made of aluminum instead of cast-iron. The engine is positioned in the car's trunk and can only be accessed from inside the car.

YEAR 2009

ORIGIN India

ENGINE 624 cc, straight-two

TOP SPEED 65 mph (105 kph)

Hyundai i20

With features including six airbags and a braking system that reduces the risk of skidding, the Hyundai i20 has a high safety rating.

YEAR 2008

ORIGIN South Korea

ENGINE 1,197 cc, straight-four

TOP SPEED 96 mph (154 kph)

Headlights can automatically sense darkness

BMW 530d Gran Turismo

The combination of the stylish features of a sedan and the sporty look of a coupe gives this car a unique look. An automatic feature turns the engine off when the car stops, saving fuel.

YEAR 2010

ORIGIN Germany

ENGINE 2,993 cc, straight-six

TOP SPEED 153 mph (246 kph)

Mercedes-Benz A 250

The first Mercedes-Benz A-Class was produced in 1997. The 2012 edition, Mercedes-Benz A 250, is longer, wider, and lower than most of the earlier models. It has a spacious interior and a big trunk.

YEAR	2012
ORIGIN	Germany
ENGINE	1,991 cc, straight-four
TOP SPEED	149 mph (240 kph)

Sporty, "shooting brake" design combines features of an estate and a coupe

Sliding sunroof made of glass

A special "Attention Assist" system can detect if the driver is feeling sleepy and sound an alert.

Convertibles

A convertible car has a movable roof, or top, which means it can be changed from a closed-top to an open-top model. This feature is controlled either manually or automatically.

FOCUS ON...
TOPS
Convertibles have one of two types of roof: a hard top or a soft top.

Mazda MX-5

Inspired by the design of British sports cars in the 1960s, the Mazda MX-5 was one of the most successful convertibles of its time. It is famous for its "pop-up" headlights, which lift up from the hood when in use.

YEAR	1989
ORIGIN	Japan
ENGINE	1,597 cc, straight-four
TOP SPEED	114 mph (183 kph)

"Pop-up" headlights

Lotus Elise

This stylish, two-seater convertible is recognized by its distinct "bug-eyed" headlights. Its bonded aluminum chassis and fiberglass panels help to reduce both its weight and the cost. At 1,600 lb (725 kg), it weighs half as much as an average saloon.

YEAR	1996
ORIGIN	UK
ENGINE	1,796 cc, straight-four
TOP SPEED	150 mph (240 kph)

▲ A hard top is made out of a rigid material, such as plastic, steel, or aluminum. A car may have a detachable (removable) or a retractable (foldable) hard top.

▲ A soft top is made out of a tough fabric, such as canvas or vinyl. The fabric is mounted on a folding frame.

Aston Martin DB9 Volante

This soft-top Aston Martin comes with a safety feature called "roll-hoops," which protect the occupants if the car were to roll over. These hoops are hidden in the rear headrests and pop out when sensors detect that the car might face an accident.

YEAR	2011
ORIGIN	UK
ENGINE	5,935 cc, V12
TOP SPEED	306 mph (190 kph)

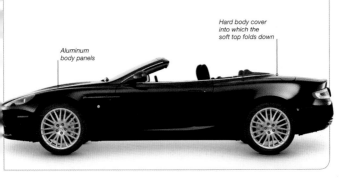

Hard body cover into which the soft top folds down

Aluminum body panels

Infiniti G37 Convertible

The hard top of the Infiniti G37 is made up of three hinged panels. When the top goes down, these panels fold into the trunk, leaving little space for anything else.

YEAR	2009
ORIGIN	Japan
ENGINE	3,696 cc, V6

TOP SPEED 155 mph (250 kph)

Volkswagen Golf Cabriolet MK6

The design of this convertible is based on the hatchback version of the Volkswagen Golf. Its folding fabric top can open in only 9.5 seconds, even when the car is driven at a speed of 19 mph (30 kph).

YEAR	2011
ORIGIN	Germany
ENGINE	2,480 cc, straight-five

TOP SPEED 130 mph (209 kph)

Porsche 911 Carrera S Cabriolet

The Porsche 911 Carrera S Cabriolet has an electronic screen, called a "wind-deflector," which pops up behind the rear seats. It cuts down wind and noise levels in the car when the top is down.

YEAR	2012
ORIGIN	Germany
ENGINE	3,800 cc, flat-six

TOP SPEED 187 mph (301 kph)

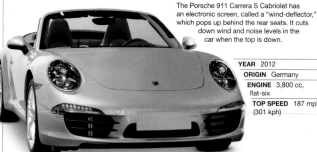

Electrically operated, folding fabric roof

Chevrolet Corvette Stingray Convertible C7

This convertible has an aluminum frame that makes it 100 lb (45 kg) lighter than previous, steel-framed models. The soft top also reduces weight.

YEAR	2014
ORIGIN	USA
ENGINE	6,200 cc, V8
TOP SPEED	180 mph (290 kph)

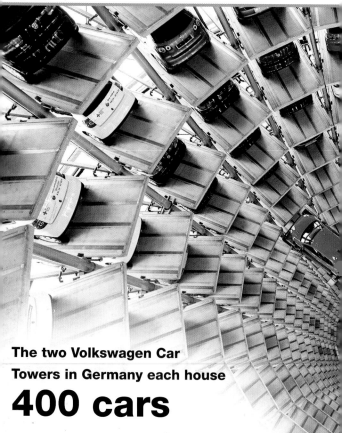

The two Volkswagen Car

Towers in Germany each house

400 cars

CAR TOWERS
The cars produced at the world's largest car factory—Autostadt, in Germany—are stored in the two 20-story Volkswagen Car Towers. The cars from the factory are delivered on a conveyor belt and moved around the tower by elevator. Cars can travel up and down the tower at a speed of 4.5 mph (7 kph).

Coupes

In the 19th century, coupes were horse-drawn carriages with a seat for two people. Today, the word "coupe" refers to a car with at least two seats, and, typically, two doors and a fixed, sloping roof. Some also come in hatchback and four-door versions.

Audi TTS

Light and fast, the Audi TTS comes with a magnetic suspension system, which adapts to uneven road surfaces for a smoother ride.

YEAR	2008
ORIGIN	Hungary
ENGINE	1,984 cc, straight-four
TOP SPEED	155 mph (250 kph)

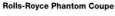

Rolls-Royce Phantom Coupe

The aluminum body of the Phantom Coupe is lightweight but strong. The car shares many features with its saloon version, such as a luxurious interior and powerful engine. Its doors are hinged at the rear rather than front. The navigation cameras give a 360-degree view of the surroundings, making parking and reversing easier.

YEAR	2008
ORIGIN	UK
ENGINE	6,752 cc, V12
TOP SPEED	155 mph (250 kph)

Bentley Continental GT Speed

The front grille of the Bentley Continental GT Speed has been designed to improve engine cooling. The smaller-than-usual steering wheel makes it easy to manoeuvre the car.

YEAR 2007

ORIGIN UK

ENGINE 5,998 cc, W12

TOP SPEED 202 mph (325 kph)

FOCUS ON...
TRUNK LIDS

The design of the trunk lid in station wagons varies. It can be hinged at the top, side, or bottom.

▲ In a split-gate trunk lid, the rear window swings upward and the lower lid downward.

▲ As the name suggests, a side-hinge trunk lid has a single door that is hinged on the side.

▲ A dual-hinge trunk lid has a pair of doors that are hinged on each side, and open outward.

Station wagons

A station wagon is a type of sedan with a roof that extends to the rear. Unlike a sedan, it does not have a separate trunk. Instead, there is a space behind the rows of seats where luggage can be kept, which can be accessed through a rear door.

Mercedes-Benz E-Class W124

The Mercedes-Benz E-Class W124 has an aerodynamic design that reduces fuel consumption. It has only one windshield wiper, but it can reach to most of the windshield.

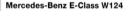

The W124 is a well-made car that typically lasts for up to 300,000 miles (500,000 km).

YEAR	1985
ORIGIN	Germany
ENGINE	4,192 cc, V8
TOP SPEED	155 mph (250 kph)

Jaguar X-type Sportwagon

Hooded, oval headlights

The first station wagon created by Jaguar, this car is based on the X-type sedan. However, the rear doors and body structure are fully redesigned. To avoid the typical "boxy" look of a station wagon, the roof is made to slope down toward the rear.

YEAR	2004
ORIGIN	UK
ENGINE	2,967 cc, V6
TOP SPEED	122 mph (196 kph)

Ford Mondeo Mk IV

The windshield of the fourth generation Ford Mondeo is designed to keep out the Sun's heat. Its front grille vent opens when the car is being driven, to keep the engine cool. Once the car picks up speed, the vent closes.

YEAR	2007
ORIGIN	Germany
ENGINE	2,261 cc, straight-four
TOP SPEED	121 mph (195 kph)

BMW Mini Clubman

The BMW Mini Clubman has a dual-hinge boot lid and an extra "club door" on the driver's side, which is hinged from the rear. The club door can be opened after the front door to make it easier to get to the rear seats.

YEAR	2008
ORIGIN	UK
ENGINE	1,598 cc, four-cylinder
TOP SPEED	125 mph (201 kph)

Ford Focus ST Wagon

This station wagon's unique Sport Steering System helps the driver to turn by increasing the sensitivity of the steering wheel. This feature is also useful when parking in tight spaces.

YEAR	2012
ORIGIN	Germany
ENGINE	2,500 cc, straight-five
TOP SPEED	154 mph (248 kph)

Mercedes-Benz CLS Shooting Brake

The spacious Shooting Brake was the second car in the world, after the Mercedes CLS, to have LED headlights, which use less energy and are brighter than standard bulbs.

Audi A6 Avant

The 2011 Audi A6 Avant consumes 18 percent less fuel than the previous model of the car. This is because its chassis is made mainly of aluminum, which makes it lighter in weight.

YEAR	2011
ORIGIN	Germany
ENGINE	2,995 cc, V6
TOP SPEED	155 mph (250 kph)

YEAR	2012
ORIGIN	Germany
ENGINE	4,633 cc, V8
TOP SPEED	155 mph (250 kph)

Hyundai i30 Wagon

The Hyundai i30 Wagon has a spacious interior and can carry more luggage than the model's hatchback version. It even has an underfloor compartment for extra storage space.

YEAR	2013
ORIGIN	South Korea
ENGINE	1,591 cc, straight-four
TOP SPEED	119 mph (192 kph)

Minivans

Also known as multipurpose vehicles (MPVs), minivans are tall, spacious cars that can carry five to eight passengers. Like the front row, the middle and back rows are often made up of individual seats, which can be folded or removed.

Mitsubishi Space Wagon

This was one of the first minivans. It came in five- and seven-seat versions. It was sold under different names, including the Chariot, the Nimbus, and the Expo.

YEAR	1984
ORIGIN	Japan
ENGINE	1,725 cc, straight-four
TOP SPEED	97 mph (156 kph)

Ford Windstar

The Windstar was Ford's first minivan with front- wheel drive (where the engine's power goes to the front wheels only). Smoother performance and handling gave it an edge over other minivans of its time.

YEAR	1994
ORIGIN	USA
ENGINE	3,797 cc, V6
TOP SPEED	116 mph (187 kph)

Volkswagen Sharan

This car gets its name from a Persian word meaning "carrier of kings." Around 670,000 Sharan cars were made over 15 years.

YEAR	1995
ORIGIN	Portugal
ENGINE	2,792 cc, V6
TOP SPEED	110 mph (177 kph)

Renault Kangoo 1

The rear seats of the adaptable Renault Kangoo can be removed to make more room. Because it is a tall car, it can be used if an occupant needs to fit in a wheelchair.

YEAR	1997
ORIGIN	France
ENGINE	1,390 cc, straight-four
TOP SPEED	97 mph (156 kph)

Mercedes-Benz Viano

The minivan version of the Mercedes-Benz Vito van—the Viano—has a stylish interior, most models being equipped with storage cabinets and a folding table. It is a spacious car that comes in three different body lengths.

YEAR 2004

ORIGIN Spain

ENGINE 2,143 cc, straight-four

TOP SPEED 117 mph (188 kph)

A variant called Marco Polo has a closet, a rear seat that can be turned into a bed, and a pop-up roof for more headroom.

Indicator lights mounted on side mirrors

Volkswagen Touran

The 2006 Volkswagen Touran is an improved version of the 2003 model. One of the most interesting additions is that of ParkAssist technology, which parks the car automatically, without the driver holding the steering wheel. The ParkAssist gauges the speed and available space and avoids surrounding objects.

YEAR 2006

ORIGIN Germany

ENGINE 1,984 cc, straight-four

TOP SPEED 125 mph (200 kph)

Peugeot 5008

Peugeot's first medium-sized minivan, the 5008 is one of the more spacious, yet stylish, cars of the type. The middle seats can be folded down all the way to the floor, providing more luggage space. Top-of-the-line models have a glass roof that extends all the way to the rear.

YEAR 2009

ORIGIN France

ENGINE 1,598 cc, straight-four

TOP SPEED 121 mph (195 kph)

Chevrolet Orlando

Originally introduced as a concept car in 2008, the Chevrolet Orlando is relatively compact for a seven-seater. It has three rows of tiered seating, which allows a clear view for passengers on the back seats as they sit slightly higher than those in the front.

YEAR	2010
ORIGIN	USA
ENGINE	2,384 cc, straight-four
TOP SPEED	125 mph (200 kph)

Citroën C4 Picasso

The C4 Picasso draws on features of Citroën's recent concept cars, with LED running lights in the front and a rounded nose. Its unusual windshield creates a sense of space, and improves visibility for the driver.

Wide-angle windshield

YEAR 2013
ORIGIN France
ENGINE 1,598 cc straight-four
TOP SPEED 116 mph (187 kph)

Toyota Prius V

With the Prius V, Toyota has expanded its range of Prius hybrid (powered by gas and electricity) models to four. This one has a larger body than the other Prius models, and also features a unique roof, made of a lightweight resin, which is 40 percent lighter than a glass roof of the same size.

YEAR 2011
ORIGIN Japan
ENGINE 1,798 cc straight-four
TOP SPEED 103 mph (166 kph)

One of the Mini Coopers used in
the 2003 film *The Italian Job* had

two steering wheels

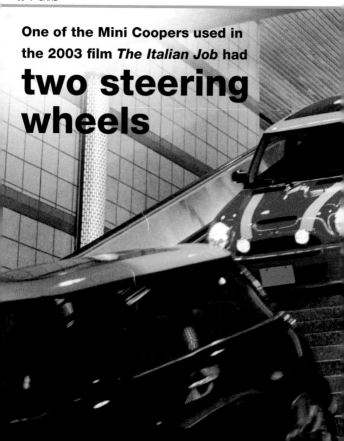

AN UNUSUAL FEATURE
Many movies feature car stunts, including car-chase scenes and car jumping stunts. For one such scene in *The Italian Job* (2003), a Mini Cooper was custom-built with two steering wheels. This helped the actors to perform while a stuntman actually drove the car.

SUVs

A sport utility vehicle (SUV) is designed to cope with driving on rough terrain. Most SUVs have four-wheel drive, in which the engine powers all four wheels instead of only the front or the rear wheels. The first SUVs were based on military vehicles.

FOCUS ON...
SIZE
SUVs can be divided into three broad groups, based on their size: mini, compact, and full-size.

Lexus GX J120

The GX J120 was Lexus's third SUV. The exterior of this eight-seater was inspired by the Toyota Land Cruiser Prado, with both cars sharing similar dimensions.

YEAR 2003

ORIGIN Japan

ENGINE 4,664 cc, V8

TOP SPEED 122 mph (197 kph)

A mini SUV, such as the Nissan Juke, is usually less than 13 ft 9 in (4.2 m) long.

▲ A compact SUV, such as the Toyota RAV4, is typically 14–15 ft (4.25–4.6 m) long.

▲ A full-sized SUV, such as the Mercedes-Benz GL Class, is usually at least 17 ft (5 m) long.

Hummer H2

The H2 was the second vehicle in the Hummer range. Just as the H1 before it, its design was based on the US military vehicle, the Humvee. The Hummer H2 has the frame of a light truck and is wider than typical city cars.

YEAR	2003
ORIGIN	USA
ENGINE	5,967 cc, V8
TOP SPEED	109 mph (176 kph)

Nissan Armada

Built on the same body framework
as Nissan's pickup truck Titan, the
Armada is a full-size SUV. It can
seat up to eight people.

YEAR 2004
ORIGIN Japan
ENGINE
5,552 cc, V8
TOP SPEED
120 mph
(193 kph)

Mercedes-Benz GL Class

The seven-seater GL boasts
a number of luxury features,
such as heated rear seats.
Larger than comparable
cars, it has a higher roof
and a huge trunk space
with a capacity of
53 gallons (200 liters).

YEAR 2006
ORIGIN Germany
ENGINE 2,987 cc, V6
TOP SPEED
124 mph (199 kph)

Jeep Patriot

One of the cheapest SUVs available in its size, this compact SUV retains all of the features of a typical Jeep, including round headlights, vertical windows, and a wide radiator grille.

YEAR	2007
ORIGIN	USA
ENGINE	1,968 cc, straight-four
TOP SPEED	117 mph (188 kph)

Chevrolet Tahoe

The Tahoe was revised in 2007 with a new hood and grille, new door panels, and new seat designs. It can seat nine people, but the third row of seats cannot fold flat. This gives it limited trunk space.

YEAR	2007
ORIGIN	USA
ENGINE	5,300 cc, V8
TOP SPEED	112 mph (180 kph)

Audi Q5

Audi's first compact SUV has an innovative roof rack with sensors that allow the car to automatically adjust its center of gravity when the rack is loaded, helping the car to stay balanced.

YEAR	2009
ORIGIN	Germany
ENGINE	2,967 cc, V6
TOP SPEED	140 mph (225 kph)

Ford Escape Hybrid

The Ford Escape was the first hybrid SUV, launched in 2004. It was given a face-lift in 2009, with added features, such as improved interior lighting and heated front seats.

YEAR	2009
ORIGIN	USA
ENGINE	2,488 cc, straight-four
TOP SPEED	102 mph (164 kph)

BMW X5 xDrive50i

The xDrive is a powerful car with a new turbocharged diesel and gas engine. The headlights and fog lights sit high and close to the radiator grille, giving it a rugged appearance. Some optional features include a Lane Departure Warning, which identifies the car's movement away from marked lanes with the help of side-mounted cameras. The steering wheel starts vibrating to alert the driver in such situations.

YEAR	2011
ORIGIN	Germany
ENGINE	4,395 cc, V8
TOP SPEED	131 mph (210 kph)

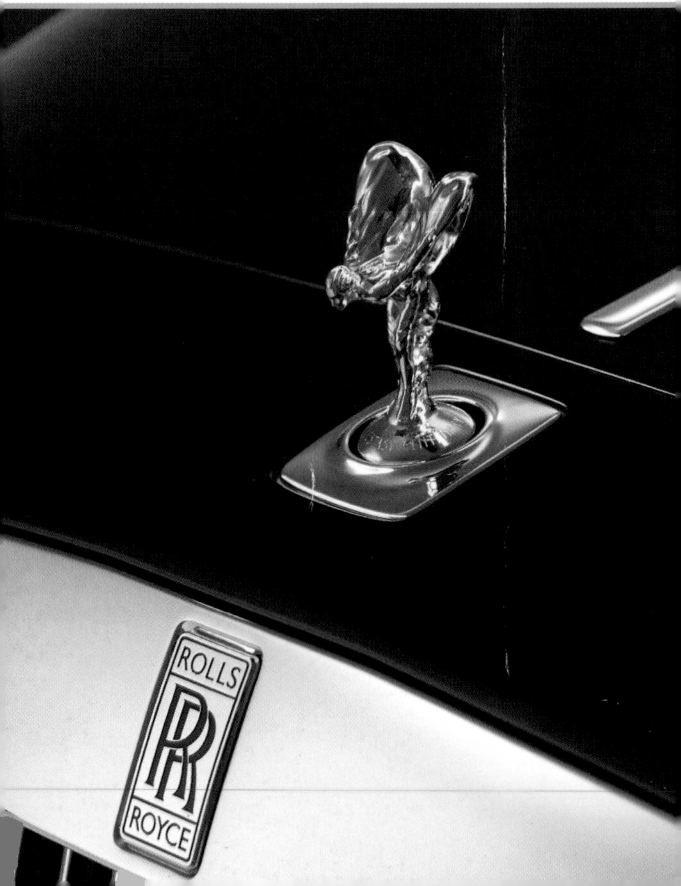
ROLLS
RR
ROYCE

Luxury cars

Luxury cars are owned as status symbols, commanding steep price tags and possessing extravagant features. Often, just a few cars of a particular model are produced, making them even more exclusive. Sometimes made-to-order, these cars promise high levels of passenger comfort, customized interiors, and an enhanced driving experience.

TRAVELING IN STYLE
Most luxury car brands provide the option of personalized accessories, such as luggage, which are often customized to match the car's interior.

Luxury cars

Luxury (top-end) cars are sleek, very expensive, high-performance machines. These exclusive vehicles are bought by wealthy people as a sign of social status. Such cars are decorated using the finest materials and come with optional extravagant features.

Interior style

The interior of a luxury car can be equipped with plush seats, made with the finest leather and fabrics, in the buyer's favorite colors. The ceiling can even be lined with crystals, as here.

Choosing the best

The privileged buyers of these fashionable cars can choose different trims, materials, colors, and expensive accessories. Some luxury cars are completely hand-built— all parts, exterior and interior, are put together manually.

YEAR 2003

ORIGIN USA

ENGINE 6,200 cc, V8

Range Rover Limousine

The stretch version of a popular SUV, the Range
Rover limousine has been designed for luxury.
It comes with a "jet door"—a door that opens
upward like the door of a small jet plane.

YEAR 2002

ORIGIN UK

ENGINE 4,999 cc, V8

Jet door

US PRESIDENTIAL LIMOUSINE
The US presidential limousine is a custom-built and heavily armored Cadillac, with doors 8 in (20 cm) thick and bulletproof windows 5 in (13 cm) thick. The trunk space contains weapons and also a supply of blood of the president's blood type, for emergencies.

OF AMERICA

The US presidential limousine has its own oxygen supply

Grand tourers

A grand tourer, or GT, is a stylish car that can be driven over long distances. It is capable of high speed, but, unlike a sports car, it has a luxurious interior built for comfort. The name refers to an 18th-century tradition of grand tours, where young people from wealthy families took a cultural tour across Europe.

Jaguar XJS V12

The sleek XJS has a padded top. With a popular two-door, full convertible style and a V12 engine, this model became one of the most successful grand tourers of its time.

YEAR	1988
ORIGIN	UK
ENGINE	5,343 cc, V12
TOP SPEED	150 mph (241 kph)

Ford Mustang GT

Automobile designer Patrick Schiavone remodeled the Mustang in 1993 to create the Ford Mustang GT. This new version boasted style elements from earlier models, and a high-performance V8 engine. It earned the title 1994 Motor Trend Car of the Year.

YEAR 1994

ORIGIN USA

ENGINE 4,942 cc, V8

TOP SPEED 136 mph (219 kph)

Porsche 911 Carrera Cabriolet

In 1998, Porsche's 911 sports car received its most significant upgrade since its launch in 1963. The latest model featured a new water-cooled engine.

YEAR 1998

ORIGIN Germany

ENGINE 3,600 cc, flat-six

TOP SPEED 170 mph (274 kph)

Curved headlight

Ferrari Enzo

Sleek side panels add to aerodynamic design

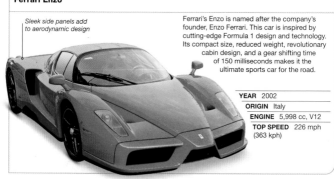

Ferrari's Enzo is named after the company's founder, Enzo Ferrari. This car is inspired by cutting-edge Formula 1 design and technology. Its compact size, reduced weight, revolutionary cabin design, and a gear shifting time of 150 milliseconds makes it the ultimate sports car for the road.

YEAR	2002
ORIGIN	Italy
ENGINE	5,998 cc, V12
TOP SPEED	226 mph (363 kph)

Pontiac GTO

The Pontiac GTO can accelerate from 0 to 60 mph (97 kph) in about 5 seconds. The addition of bright wheel spokes and a spoiler adds a sporty edge to its appearance.

YEAR	2006
ORIGIN	Australia
ENGINE	6,375 cc, V8
TOP SPEED	175 mph (282 kph)

Audi R8

The two-seater R8 uses Audi's trademark Quattro four-wheel drive system. It has an aluminum, lightweight chassis, and has a more spacious interior than other sports cars. Its superior technology and smooth ride makes it a true rival to the iconic Porsche 911.

YEAR	2006
ORIGIN	Germany
ENGINE	5,204 cc, V10
TOP SPEED	196 mph (315 kph)

Nissan GT-R SpecV

A special variant of the Nissan GT-R, the GT-R SpecV is 132 lb (60 kg) lighter than the standard version. This car features some carbon-fiber body panels, no rear seats, and a titanium exhaust—a lightweight alternative to a steel one.

YEAR	2007
ORIGIN	Japan
ENGINE	3,799 cc, V6
TOP SPEED	193 mph (311 kph)

Dodge Challenger

The long-hood design of the Challenger is a tribute to the compact, powerful American cars of the 1970s. However, its performance matches that of modern-day cars. While it offers a smooth ride and handles well, many feel the interior does not match up to the dramatic exterior.

YEAR	2008
ORIGIN	USA
ENGINE	6,059 cc, V8
TOP SPEED	145 mph (233 kph)

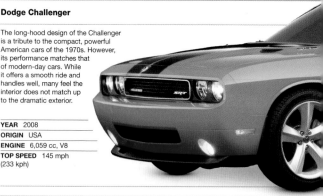

Mercedes-Benz SLS AMG

This model was the first Mercedes-Benz car to be designed in-house by its development wing—AMG. The most iconic feature of the two-door grand tourer is its "gull-wing" doors, which open upward.

YEAR	2010
ORIGIN	Germany
ENGINE	6,208 cc, V8
TOP SPEED	197 mph (317 kph)

Gull-wing doors

Chevrolet Camaro 2SS

The Camaro 2SS is known for its sleek
exterior and powerful performance. Its
short side window, small, high-mounted
taillight, and low roofline with sloping
windshield add to the appeal.

YEAR 2010
ORIGIN USA
ENGINE 6,162 cc, V8
TOP SPEED 155 mph (250 kph)

Racing and sports cars

From long-distance rallies to high-speed track-based competitions, car racing has been popular since cars first appeared. While sports cars are powerful enough to be raced occasionally if the owner wants to, race cars are set apart by their speed and design, and they are raced by highly skilled drivers.

RACING TIRES
Different tires are used for different conditions: intermediate tread tires for wet tracks; heavy tread tires for standing water; and slick tires for dry tracks.

The world of racing

The first car races were organized in the 1890s, to prove the speed and reliability of the vehicles involved. Soon it became a popular source of entertainment, and different categories of races were introduced. Today, car racing is an international sport.

Stock car racing

Stock car races are typically held on an oval track. NASCAR (National Association for Stock Car Racing) is the largest body that organizes these races. The Sprint Cup Series is the most popular NASCAR race in the United States.

Rallying

In rally races, cars run between two controlled stops (special stages) on public or private roads, instead of a track. Pairs of drivers aim to arrive first or match a stipulated time.

Drag racing

Drag racers compete in pairs on a short, standard track—usually 1,320 ft (400 m) in length. The first to cross the finish line wins.

Formula racing

Formula racing gets its name from early motor racing championships, held in Europe. These had set rules, or a "formula," that every participant had to follow. Today, formula racing includes Formula One, Two, and Three series.

Speedsters

Both racing and sports cars are built for speed, but only sports cars appear in showrooms for sale to the public. Race cars may be closed-wheel (with wings covering the wheel) or open-wheel (without wings). They are modified for competing in various championships.

Race cars

High-performance race cars are designed specifically to take part in various types of motor racing. Modifications include adding more engines, lowering the car's height, and removing the wings.

Stock car
Stock cars resemble ordinary street models but their chassis, tires, and accessories are modified for speed and safety. These cars compete in racing events such as NASCAR.

Go-kart
A small, open-wheeled car built for racing, a go-kart can reach speeds of up to 155 mph (250 kph). Some go-karts are fitted with a specially designed engine.

Formula car
Formula cars have a long hood, single seat, and open cockpit. The engine is placed behind the driver.

ir flow

rodynamics is the study of the flow of air around
moving object, such as a car. Cars are designed
h features that fight drag (air resistance) to
prove speed and reduce lift, which
uld flip a car.

Rear spoiler, or
wing, stabilizes
car at high speeds
by reducing drag

unded front wing
annels airflow
er the car

Low, flat underbody
allows smoother airflow
beneath the car

ront spoiler, or air dam,
decreases amount of air
assing underneath the car

Front air inlet can be
closed to lessen drag

ports cars

quipped with strong engines and designed
be sleek and lightweight, sports cars are
sually production vehicles (made for sale)
at provide the thrill of driving at high speeds.

Supercar
Costly supercars are
exceptional, superfast
sports cars, featuring
state-of-the-art
racing technology.

Roadster
Agile, two-seater
oadsters, such as this
BMW Z4, are usually
en-top cars. They may
ome with a soft top or
a retractable hard top.

FOCUS ON...
F1 FLAGS
In an F1 race, different flags are used to indicate the condition of the track or to relay important messages to the drivers.

▲ A red flag signals that the race has been stopped for safety reasons and that all drivers must pull in.

▲ A striped flag warns drivers of substances on the track, including water, oil, and debris.

▲ The checkered flag is shown to declare the winner and to signal that the race is officially over.

Racing cars

Built for speed and agility, racing cars are usually one- or two-seater vehicles designed to be driven in racing competitions. Cars for different types of race, such as Formula or drag racing, have specifically modified engines and body shapes.

Ferrari F138

Designed for the 2013 Formula One (F1) Season, the lightweight F138 was driven by the two-time World Champion Fernando Alonso. The name—F138—is a combination of the race year and the number of engine cylinders. The car has a high nose, while the rear is narrow, which makes it more aerodynamic.

YEAR	2013
ORIGIN	Italy
RACE	F1

Vent for air intake

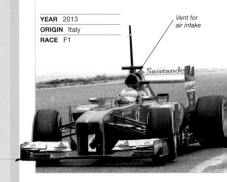

McLaren Mercedes MP4-28

Launched on January 31, 2013, as part of McLaren's 50th anniversary celebration, the MP4-28 has a completely new design—with a new chassis and a higher nose. However, it failed to perform well in the races.

YEAR 2013
ORIGIN UK
RACE F1

Rear wings

Camera mount

Radio antenna

Detachable nosepiece

Red Bull Racing RB9

The RB9 was driven by Sebastian Vettel, the three-time winner of the World Driver's Championship, which is awarded to the F1 driver of the season. This car faced the disadvantage of being equipped with tires that wore out more quickly during a race than other cars' tires.

YEAR 2013
ORIGIN UK
RACE F1

Mercedes AMG Petronas F1W05

The F1W05 has a smooth, wide nose, unlike the typical raised nose of a Formula car. The downturned nose makes the car more aerodynamic.

YEAR 2014
ORIGIN Germany
RACE F1

Camera mount on the nose

Habermann Top Methanol Dragster

This dragster (car used in drag racing) was driven by Dennis Habermann, who was third in the 2012 FIA European Drag Racing Championship. Although similar in design to Top Fuel dragsters, Top Methanols are less powerful. They are powered by fuel that is 100 percent methanol, while Top Fuel dragsters use a fuel mixture that is only 10 percent methanol.

Top Methanol Dragsters can cover a quarter mile (0.4 km) in less than 6 seconds, reaching speeds of up to 248 mph (400 kph).

YEAR	2012
ORIGIN	Germany
RACE	Top Methanol

Castrol GTX High Mileage Ford Mustang

The High Mileage Ford Mustang was driven by 16-time Funny Car race champion John Force. Funny Car dragsters look similar to production cars but have custom-built chassis. Ford Mustangs have been used in drag racing since 1964.

YEAR	2009
ORIGIN	USA
RACE	Funny Car

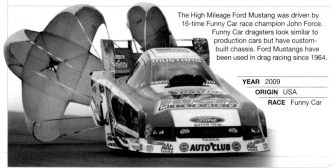

Cylinder

DENNIS

NI-FIT

talysatoren

sw.uni-fit.de

Mountain View Tire Dodge Avenger

Driven by the youngest winner of the National Hot Rod Association (NHRA) Pro Stock class, Vincent Nobile, the Dodge Avenger has been modified as per NHRA's strict regulations. Nobile reached a top speed of 211.03 mph (339.61 kph) with the Dodge Avenger.

YEAR 2012

ORIGIN USA

RACE Pro Stock

SEAT Léon

The Léon was first introduced to the World
Touring Car Championship in 2005. SEAT won the
manufacturer's title in 2008 and 2009 with this
car. A limited edition road-going model, the
Cupra World Champion Edition, was built in 2010
to celebrate the successful race season.

YEAR 2009

ORIGIN Spain

RACE World Touring Car Championship

Ford Fusion

When a NASCAR car is taking a sharp turn at
high speed, the air flowing underneath it can
lift it off the ground. The Ford Fusion has a
low and wide front bumper, which blocks
this air flow, making it safer to drive.

YEAR 2011

ORIGIN USA

RACE
NASCAR

Chevrolet Impala

Richard Childress Racing Team's Chevrolet Impala was driven by Kevin Harvick up until the 2013 season. Harvick won the race at the 2012 Phoenix International Raceway and finished third overall in the 2013 Sprint Cup Series.

YEAR 2012

ORIGIN USA

RACE NASCAR

Honda Civic

Pirtek Racing team's Honda Civic participates in the British Touring Car Championship, a race event for sedans. It is equipped with a low-cost, turbocharged engine, which matches the specifications required for all touring race cars.

YEAR 2013

ORIGIN UK

RACE British Touring Car Championship

Superkart 250 cc

The fastest go-kart in the world, a Superkart 250 cc can complete laps faster than more technologically advanced race cars. It can reach a top speed of 160 mph (257 kph), and is primarily used in the British Superkart Championship.

YEAR	Unknown
ORIGIN	Unknown
RACE	British Superkart Championship

Subaru Impreza WRC

Introduced in 1993, the Impreza WRC has performed well in rally races over the years. The 2004 model had improved aerodynamics, a turbocharged engine, and four-wheel drive (where the engine's power goes to the front and rear wheels).

YEAR	2004
ORIGIN	Japan
RACE	World Rally Racing

Swamp Thing

The Swamp Thing is a monster truck, which is a modified pickup truck with giant wheels. This vehicle weighs a hefty 11,000 lb (5,000 kg). In addition to competing in monster truck races, it also participates in entertainment events, such as crushing smaller cars and performing stunts.

YEAR 2004

ORIGIN UK

RACE Monster truck racing

Ferrari's fastest ever pit stop took just

1.95 seconds

PIT STOP

A race car makes a pit stop to get new tires and have minor repairs between laps. Pit stops are in a lane that runs parallel to the race track. The team's pit crew must complete all the tasks as fast as possible for the car to get back in the race. An average F1 pit stop lasts about 2.5 seconds.

Roadsters

Traditionally, a roadster was defined as a car with no windows and, sometimes, no doors. Today, however, a roadster is any two-seater convertible, open-top car (without a fixed roof). This sporty car has a lightweight structure, and can have a soft top or a hard top.

BMW Z1

The Z1 was BMW's first open two-seater since the late 1950s. A unique feature of this car is that its doors can be retracted vertically down into the car's body. The body itself is high enough to offer protection even when the doors are down.

YEAR	1989
ORIGIN	Germany
ENGINE	2,494 cc, six-cylinder
TOP SPEED	140 mph (225 kph)

All BMW Z1s were left-hand drive, except the final one, which was also the only Z1 to be hand-built.

Marcos Mantula Spyder

The Spyder is the convertible version of the 1984 Marcos Mantula coupe. Technologically, the two cars are similar, except that the Spyder has a stiffer chassis to make up for the open roof. It also has a rounded nose and a padded soft top.

YEAR	1986
ORIGIN	UK
ENGINE	3,532 cc, V8
TOP SPEED	139 mph (224 kph)

Alfa Romeo Spider

The Alfa Romeo Spider has a typical Italian design, with a low body that is broad and flattened. It is fitted with the trademark Alfa Romeo grille, round headlights, and has a steeply sloping windshield. Although it has a high rear, the hood space is small.

YEAR	1995
ORIGIN	Italy
ENGINE	2,959 cc, V6
TOP SPEED	140 mph (225 kph)

Renault Sport Spider

Built to promote Renault as a sporting
brand, the Sport Spider is a lightweight
car with an aluminum chassis and a
plastic body. It has neither a roof nor
a top and only Sport Spiders sold in
the UK have a windshield.

YEAR	1996
ORIGIN	France
ENGINE	1,998 cc, straight-four
TOP SPEED	131 mph (211 kph)

Honda S2000 AP1

First shown as a concept car in 1995,
the S2000 AP1 was launched in 1999.
This stylish car is equipped with a vinyl
soft top. An aluminum hard top is
available as an optional extra.

YEAR	1999
ORIGIN	Japan
ENGINE	1,997 cc, straight-four
TOP SPEED	150 mph (241 kph)

Lamborghini Murcièlago Roadster

Fighter aircraft, Spanish architecture, and
mega-yachts were among the things that
inspired the styling of this impressive, soft-top
Lamborghini. The Murcièlago has a low-tech,
manually operated roof.

YEAR 2004

ORIGIN Italy

ENGINE 6,496 cc, V12

TOP SPEED 200 mph (322 kph)

Audi TT RS Roadster

The TT RS is equipped with an engine designed exclusively for it, and no other Audi car used it until the RS3 in 2011. This powerful engine, combined with the lightweight aluminum chassis and body, provides a smooth ride.

YEAR 2009

ORIGIN Germany

ENGINE 2,479 cc, straight-five

TOP SPEED 155 mph (250 kph)

Supercars

Supercars are very expensive sports cars. They are usually produced in limited numbers, which makes them exclusive and highly prized. Equipped with the latest technology, these powerful performers are capable of reaching extremely high speeds.

Ferrari 288 GTO

Originally built for racing, the 288 GTO did not end up on the track, as the race category it was designed for was discontinued. This limited edition car was released only in Ferrari's iconic red color.

YEAR	1984
ORIGIN	Italy
ENGINE	2,855 cc, V8
TOP SPEED	190 mph (306 kph)

Aston Martin V8 Zagato

Recognized for its unique angular design, the V8 Zagato is one of the rarest supercars. Aston Martin decided to make only 52 cars of this model, and all of them were bought before its production, solely on the basis of drawings and a scale model.

YEAR	1986
ORIGIN	UK
ENGINE	5,340 cc, V8
TOP SPEED	186 mph (300 kph)

McLaren F1

In its time, the McLaren F1 succeeded in breaking multiple speed records. It can reach such high speeds that its engine compartment has to be lined with gold foil, to shield against the heat produced.

YEAR 1992
ORIGIN UK
ENGINE
6,064 cc, V12
TOP SPEED
243 mph
(391 kph)

Lamborghini Diablo VT Roadster

With this car, Lamborghini continued its tradition of naming its models after fighting bulls. The Diablo VT Roadster was a convertible version of the coupe. It earned its supercar status as it was one of the fastest cars of its time.

YEAR 1995
ORIGIN Italy
ENGINE 5,707 cc, V12
TOP SPEED
201 mph (323 kph)

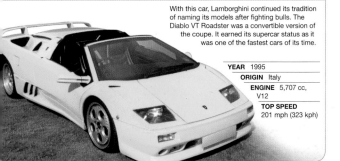

Alfa Romeo 8C Competizione

This car's design was inspired by the Alfa Romeo models of the 1950s and 1960s. Its name is a tribute to Alfa Romeo's racing tradition: "8C" is a reference to the eight-cylinder engine used by most Alfa Romeo race cars in the 1930s, and "Competizione" is Italian for "competition."

YEAR 2007

ORIGIN Italy

ENGINE 4,591 cc, V8

TOP SPEED
181 mph (292 kph)

Lamborghini Aventador LP 700-4

Parts of this sleek two-seater's body, including the roof and doors, are made of carbon fiber. While this makes the car body extremely strong, the use of aluminum in other parts makes the Aventador light as well.

YEAR 2011

ORIGIN Italy

ENGINE 6,498 cc, V12

TOP SPEED 217 mph (350 kph)

Bugatti Veyron 16.4 Grand Sport

One of the fastest and most expensive
convertibles in the world, this supercar has
two removable roofs. One of them is a
manually removable hard top, made of
transparent polycarbonate. The
other is a soft top that unfolds
over the cabin, much like
a flat umbrella.

YEAR	2009
ORIGIN	France
ENGINE	7,993 cc, W16
TOP SPEED	253 mph (407 kph)

**The Bugatti Veyron
Super Sport was the world's**

fastest road car

**for three years, with a
top speed of 267.8 mph (431 kph)**

MADE FOR SPEED
Bugatti's supercar, recognized by its iconic horseshoe-shaped front grille, was named after the French race car driver Pierre Veyron. This car takes only 2.5 seconds to reach a speed of 60 mph (97 kph). Its record was broken by the Hennessey Venom GT in February 2014.

Amazing cars

Some cars are set apart by their unusual designs or extremely powerful engines, while others look to change the concept of what a car is or how it can be run. Record breakers, usually jet-propelled, show how fast a car can go, while amphibious cars make it possible to drive cars through water. Several cars are built purely as concepts to show off advanced technologies and designs.

ELECTRIC CARS
Some cars—such as this Venturi Fétish, the world's first two-seater electric sports car—run only on electricity, using energy stored in batteries.

Out of the ordinary

In the history of car design and technology, a few special vehicles mark significant breakthroughs. These cars led the way with innovations in speed, fuel efficiency, safety, styling, or mechanics. Some vehicles are even designed for use in outer space!

Eco cars

Environmentally friendly cars are built from sustainable materials where possible and produce low or zero emissions. This all-electric BMW i3 is powered by a rechargeable battery.

Speed demons

Supersonic cars, such as the Bloodhound SSC, are designed to travel faster than the speed of sound. Powered by both a jet and a rocket engine, this car is in development to shatter the world land speed record by achieving a speed just over 1,000 mph (1,600 kph).

On land and water
Versatile and fun, amphibious vehicles, such as the WaterCar Panther, can cruise highways, climb sand dunes, or jet along a river faster than a motor cruiser.

Concept cars
Prototype cars showcase new strategies in design and technology. Previewed in 2011, this state-of-the-art hybrid Ford Evos featured many new design concepts, such as front and rear gull-wing doors.

Front gull-wing door

LED strip headlights

CARS IN SPACE
Space cars, or rovers, are built for space exploration. NASA's *Curiosity*, shown here, is controlled from Earth and conducts scientific experiments on Mars, collecting rock samples and photographing the terrain.

Hybrid cars

Cars that use more than one power source—
usually a combination of a gas engine and an
electric motor—are called hybrid cars. These
vehicles are more fuel efficient and emit
(give out) lower levels of air pollutants.

FOCUS ON...
REFUELING
In addition to gas or
diesel, hybrid cars are
powered by an electric
motor or an alternative
fuel, such as hydrogen.

Honda Insight

The Honda Insight is equipped with an electric
motor that boosts the performance of its gas
engine. In addition to the hybrid drive system,
its lightweight body and streamlined design also
help to improve the car's fuel efficiency.

YEAR	2000
ORIGIN	Japan
ENGINE	995 cc, straight-three
TOP SPEED	106 mph (170 kph)

*Most of the body is
made up of aluminum
and plastic*

Saturn Vue Green Line

The first hybrid SUV created by General
Motors, the Saturn Vue Green Line is a mild
hybrid. This means that the electric motor is
used to assist the main engine but cannot
be used independently. This model uses up to
20 percent less fuel than a regular Saturn Vue.

YEAR	2007
ORIGIN	USA
ENGINE	2,376 cc, straight-four
TOP SPEED	100 mph (160 kph)

◄ Charging points can be used to recharge the batteries of an electric hybrid car.

◄ Although not as common as charging points, hydrogen filling stations have been opened in many countries.

Toyota Prius

The 1997 Toyota Prius was the first hybrid car to be mass-produced. The 2004 Prius is a full hybrid, which means that power from the gas engine and the electric motor can be shared to run the car.

YEAR	2004
ORIGIN	Japan
ENGINE	1,497 cc, four-cylinder
TOP SPEED	106 mph (170 kph)

Toyota Highlander

The midsized SUV Highlander is a full hybrid, known for its smooth ride and spacious interior. However, it is more expensive than other SUV hybrids, and not particularly fuel efficient in comparison to other cars of the same type.

YEAR 2007

ORIGIN Japan

ENGINE 3,310 cc, straight-six

TOP SPEED 112 mph (180 kph)

Chevrolet Volt

Introduced as a concept vehicle in 2007, the Volt is a full hybrid, plug-in electric car. The electric battery is powerful enough for city driving. The Volt also has a gas-powered engine, which can be used for longer distances.

YEAR 2011

ORIGIN USA

ENGINE 1,398 cc, straight-four

TOP SPEED 100 mph (161 kph)

LaFerrari

The LaFerrari's design is inspired by the brand's race cars. Only 499 units of this sports car are planned. Unlike most hybrid vehicles, the internal combustion engine and the electric motor of the LaFerrari can run at the same time.

Nissan Cima

The luxury saloon Cima combines powerful engine performance with elegant design and a spacious interior. Its efficient hybrid technology significantly reduces the harmful emissions produced.

YEAR 2012

ORIGIN Japan

ENGINE 3,498 cc, V6

TOP SPEED 93 mph (150 kph)

YEAR 2013

ORIGIN Italy

ENGINE 6,262 cc, V12

TOP SPEED 218 mph (350 kph)

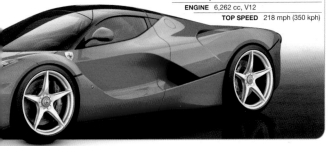

Record breakers

The first land speed record—the highest speed by a vehicle on land—was set in 1898 by Count Gaston de Chasseloup-Laubat, who drove 0.6 miles (1 km) in 57 seconds, in an electric motor-powered vehicle. Modern-day record breakers use rocket or jet engines.

Blue Flame

Driven by American race car driver Gary Gabelich, the rocket-powered Blue Flame achieved a world land speed record on the Bonneville Salt Flats in Utah on October 23, 1970. This record remained unbroken until October 1983.

YEAR	1970
ORIGIN	USA
SPEED	630.4 mph (1,015 kph)
LENGTH	37 ft 5 in (11.4 m)

Thrust2

After Thrust1 crashed in 1977, its driver Richard Noble improved the design and went on to build, and pilot, Thrust2. On October 4, 1983, Thrust2 broke Blue Flame's world land speed record. It was powered by a single Rolls-Royce Avon turbojet engine.

YEAR	1983
ORIGIN	UK
SPEED	633.5 mph (1,019.4 kph)
LENGTH	27 ft 3 in (8.3 m)

Body design is strong and rigid to withstand high speeds

ThrustSSC

ThrustSSC was the first supersonic car—one designed to be faster than the speed of sound. On October 15, 1997, it became the first car officially to break the sound barrier, and currently holds the world land speed record.

YEAR	1997
ORIGIN	UK
SPEED	763.04 mph (1,227.98 kph)
LENGTH	54 ft (16.5 m)

ThrustSSC's two engines burn nearly 5 gallons (18 liters) of fuel per second.

Bloodhound SSC

Bloodhound SSC is a supersonic car currently being developed with the goal of beating the current land speed record. This pencil-shaped car is powered by a jet engine and a rocket.

YEAR	2014
ORIGIN	UK
SPEED	About 1,000 mph (1,600 kph)
LENGTH	44 ft (13.5 m)

FOCUS ON...
DIVERSITY
Various types of vehicle
are specifically built to be
amphibious, while some
are modified for such use.

Amphibious cars

Amphibious cars can travel both on land and on or even under water. Most land vehicles can be adapted for driving on water by fitting them with a waterproof body. Some use propellers to move forward, while others use high-powered water jets.

▲ Amphibious buses are used for city sightseeing trips, carrying tourists on both roads and rivers.

▲ Amphibious boats can be used for tourism in places where there is a need to cross both land and water.

▲ Armored amphibious military tanks are used for defense and patrol work.

Amphicar Model 770

The Amphicar was the first amphibious car to be mass produced. A pair of propellers were mounted under the rear bumper to push it through water. This car steered with its front wheels not just on land, but even in water.

YEAR	1961
ORIGIN	Germany
ENGINE	1,147 cc, straight-four
TOP SPEED	Land: 70 mph (110 kph); Water: 7 mph (11 kph)

In 1965, four Englishmen crossed the English Channel in two Amphicars in just seven hours.

Gibbs Aquada

Once the Gibbs Aquada enters the water, its wheels retract, its road lights change to water lights, and a powerful jet is started to push it through the water. The entire process takes only four seconds. This three-seater car has no doors, which helps to prevent leaks.

YEAR	2003
ORIGIN	New Zealand
ENGINE	2,500 cc, V6
TOP SPEED	Land: 100 mph (161 kph); Water: 35 mph (56 kph)

WaterCar Python

In 2010, the WaterCar Python became the fastest amphibious vehicle in the world. However, it never went into production. Watercar has now built the Panther, an amphibious SUV with specifications similar to that of the Python.

YEAR	2009
ORIGIN	USA
ENGINE	2,997 cc, V6
TOP SPEED	Land: 125 mph (201 kph); Water: 60 mph (97 kph)

Cars in space

Scientists have developed special machines that have been driven on the surface of the Moon and Mars. Most of these vehicles, called rovers, are operated remotely from Earth and send back scientific data for scientists to study.

Lunokhod 1

This was one of two rovers built and sent to the Moon by the Soviet Union (a group of states that included modern-day Russia). It was controlled by radio signals from Earth and returned more than 20,000 images from the Moon in just 10 months.

SIZE	4 ft 6 in (1.35 m) tall
WEIGHT	1,665 lb (756 kg)
LAUNCH DATE	November 10, 1970

Lunar Roving Vehicle

The first rover to be driven on the Moon (rather than being controlled remotely) was a battery-powered vehicle that could carry two astronauts and their equipment. It traveled at a top speed of 11.5 mph (18.5 kph). Three such rovers were built, one for each of the last three missions to the Moon.

SIZE	10 ft (3 m) long
WEIGHT	465 lb (210 kg)
LAUNCH DATE	First launched with *Apollo 15* on July 26, 1971

Sojourner

The first rover to be operated on another planet, *Sojourner* was powered by solar panels arranged on its top and could travel at the speed of ½ in (1 cm) per second. It sent back information about the chemical makeup of the rocks on Mars, and the wind and weather conditions there.

SIZE 25½ in (65 cm) long

WEIGHT 23 lb (10.6 kg)

LAUNCH DATE December 4, 1996

Wind sensors on top of antenna

The rover was named after Sojourner Truth, a woman who traveled across North America to fight for women's rights.

Solar panels

Opportunity

In 2003, NASA sent two identical rovers—*Opportunity* and *Spirit*—to Mars with the goal of collecting and studying the Martian soil for signs of life. Both rovers could travel at a maximum speed of 2 in (50 mm) per second. Communication from *Spirit* ended in 2010, but *Opportunity* continues to send back data.

SIZE	5 ft 4 in (1.6 m) long
WEIGHT	385 lb (174 kg)
LAUNCH DATE	July 7, 2003

The spacecraft that carried *Curiosity* to Mars took 253 days to cover the 352 million miles (566 million km) between Earth and Mars.

Camera on top of mast can rotate 360 degrees

Gold-painted body helps to maintain temperature

Curiosity

This six-wheeled rover is about the same size as a small SUV. It carries equipment that can collect and analyze rock and soil samples. *Curiosity* is designed to drive over obstacles up to 25 in (65 cm) high and can travel about 660 ft (200 m) every day. It has a top speed of 1½ in (4 cm) per second.

SIZE	10 ft (3 m) long
WEIGHT	2,000 lb (900 kg)
LAUNCH DATE	November 26, 2011

Antenna

Strong outer body protects computer and electronic systems

Each wheel can move independently, making it easy to steer the rover over rough surfaces

A fully charged battery can power a solar car for up to

250 miles

(400 km)

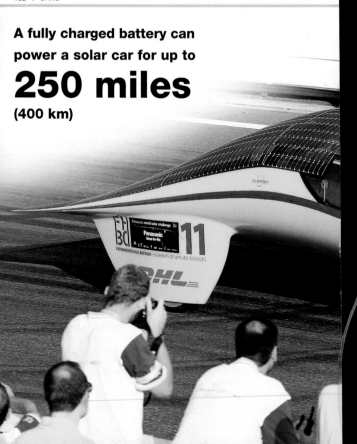

Some modern cars are powered by solar energy (energy from the Sun). These cars are covered in solar panels, which absorb and convert the Sun's energy into electricity. Some solar cars, such as the Solarworld No.1 (shown here), are built to take part in races.

Concept cars

A car created to feature an unusual new design or exciting technology is called a concept car. Concept cars are usually shown at major car shows to test new ideas and attract attention. They are one-of-a-kind models that may or may not be built for sale.

Volvo YCC

Special paint does not allow dirt to cling on easily

Gull-wing door

The YCC (Your Concept Car) is the first concept car to be designed by an all-female team. The front is lower and the rear slants back more than a typical Volvo, allowing the driver to see all four corners of the car. Other features include run-flat tires that last for a safe distance even after a puncture.

YEAR	2004
ORIGIN	Sweden
TOP SPEED	Not stated

Mercedes-Benz F700

This large sedan is powered by a new DiesOtto engine, which combines the fuel efficiency of a diesel engine with the low emissions of a gas engine. The vehicle has two laser scanners to detect uneven surfaces, allowing the car to adjust for a smoother ride.

YEAR 2008

ORIGIN Germany

TOP SPEED
125 mph
(200 kph)

Mercedes-Benz F-Cell Roadster

Inspired by the 1886 Mercedes-Benz Motorwagen, this concept car's design resembles that of a horseless carriage. This hydrogen-electric hybrid produces no harmful emissions. Other features include a joystick instead of a steering wheel, and big spoked wheels with thin, solid rubber rims.

YEAR 2009

ORIGIN Germany

TOP SPEED
15 mph (25 kph)

Cadillac Urban Luxury Concept

The Urban Luxury can seat four people despite its compact size—it is just 151 in (384 cm) long and 57 (145 cm) tall. Instead of the usual gauges, this gas-electric hybrid has touchpad screens, which can also be controlled using a voice recognition system.

YEAR 2010

ORIGIN USA

TOP SPEED Not stated

Volvo Air Motion Concept

Designed to weigh less than 1,000 lb (454 kg), this car has a simple design with fewer and lighter body parts than other cars. Instead of an internal combustion engine, it is powered by compressed air motors, which further reduces the weight.

YEAR 2010

ORIGIN Sweden

TOP SPEED Not stated

Mercedes-Benz Biome

With the help of special hybrid technology, the Biome releases oxygen instead of carbon dioxide. The car's body is made of a material called BioFibre, which is grown in a laboratory.

YEAR 2010

ORIGIN Germany

TOP SPEED Not stated

Jaguar C-X75

This two-seater supercar has four electric motors, each turning one wheel. The electric motors are powered by a gas turbine instead of a conventional piston engine. In 2011, Jaguar announced production of the C-X75 in collaboration with the Williams F1 racing team. However, production was canceled in 2012.

YEAR 2010

ORIGIN UK

TOP SPEED 205 mph (330 kph)

Aluminum body, with a carbon-fiber chassis

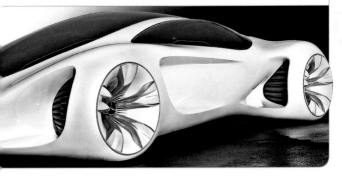

BMW i8 Concept

The futuristic BMW i8 is powered by a gas engine and an electric motor. The interior of this eco-friendly car is made up mainly of recycled material. Instead of LED headlights, it uses new laser technology that is a thousand times more powerful.

Butterfly doors open up and out

YEAR 2011

ORIGIN Germany

TOP SPEED 155 mph (250 kph)

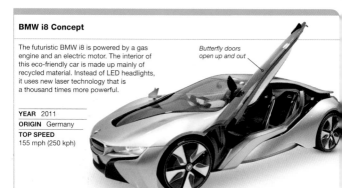

Jaguar C-X16

This is the smallest Jaguar since 1954. Its gas engine and electric motor can be used independently or together. A button on the steering wheel allows the driver to boost the engine's performance with the electric motor.

YEAR 2011

ORIGIN UK

TOP SPEED 186 mph (300 kph)

Audi Urban Concept

This ultralight two-seater concept car has a carbon fiber body, weighing just under 1,100 lb (500 kg). The driver can adjust the steering wheel and pedals to his own body measurements in this narrow car. Despite the size, the Urban Concept also has a small, drawerlike luggage compartment.

YEAR 2011

ORIGIN Germany

TOP SPEED 62 mph (100 kph)

Driver's seat is placed 12 in (30 cm) ahead of the passenger's seat to give more elbow and shoulder room

Protective mudguards on wheels, which stand away from chassis

Toyota Fun-Vii Concept

This car's exterior and interior color and design can be changed to suit the driver's mood. The Fun-Vii also has a pop-up avatar projected from the dashboard to help the driver understand the car's futuristic features. The car seats three people.

LED-screen exterior can be used as a display, with changing wallpapers

YEAR 2011

ORIGIN
Japan

TOP SPEED
Not stated

Lexus LF-LC

The Lexus Future-Luxury Coupé features an enormous front grille and day-running headlights— each shaped like an "L." The car is also equipped with a race car-inspired steering wheel and touchscreens for controlling the windows and adjusting the seats.

YEAR 2012

ORIGIN Japan

TOP SPEED Not stated

Audi Sport Quattro Concept

Designed to celebrate the 30th anniversary of the first Audi Sport Quattro model, this sporty concept car's body is mostly made up of carbon fiber, while the doors are aluminum.

YEAR 2013

ORIGIN Germany

TOP SPEED 190 mph (305 kph)

Toyota i-Road

The three-wheeled, electric-powered i-Road can seat two people, one behind the other. It has a meter that calculates how much the driver is leaning when taking a turn, and limits the angle of the turn. This ensures the car never tips over. The steering wheel vibrates to let the driver know when the car is tilting at its maximum angle.

YEAR 2013

ORIGIN Japan

TOP SPEED 37 mph (60 kph)

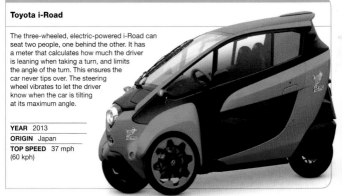

Fun cars

Some cars are truly unique, with very unusual designs. While many of these cars are modified for fun, or specially built by companies for promoting their goods, a few are based on the designer's own ideas about what a car is and what it could do.

Dusty Dave the Dolphin

Dusty Dave is an adapted 1972 Volkswagen Beetle. Its exterior was modified by sculptor Tom Kennedy so that it looked like a dolphin. Its mouth is hinged to open.

YEAR	1996
ORIGIN	USA

DESIGNED BY
Penny Smith and Harry Leverette

Ford 1932 Hot Rod

This Ford 1932 Model B has been redesigned more recently as a hot rod car, with its hood removed to show off the engine. A hot rod is fitted with a modified, powerful engine and is often painted in bright colors that add to its appeal.

YEAR	1932
ORIGIN	USA

DESIGNED BY
Unknown

Wienermobile

Shaped like a hot dog on a bun, the Wienermobile is used by the Oscar Mayer Company to advertise its products. The first Wienermobile was built in 1936, and six tour the US today. This 2004 model has gull-wing doors, a hot dog-shaped dashboard, and mustard- and ketchup-colored seats. The drivers of these cars are called "hotdoggers."

YEAR 2004
ORIGIN USA
DESIGNED BY Prototype Source

Wenzhou shoe car

Built by a shoe company to promote its brand, this shoe-shaped electric car is made of the same leather the company uses for its footwear. It took six months to construct this car, which is 10 ft (3 m) long and 3 ft (1 m) high.

YEAR 2011
ORIGIN China
DESIGNED BY Kang Shoe Company

Wind-powered car

This wind-powered car runs on two sets of generators and batteries that are connected to a fan in the front. As the car moves, the fan spins, producing electricity for the vehicle. Solar panels at the back also help generate electricity.

YEAR 2012
ORIGIN China
DESIGNED BY Tang Zhenping

Fan   Solar panels

The Rinspeed sQuba is the
first car that not only runs
on roads, but can also travel
underwater

UNDERWATER CAR
Inspired by a futuristic car in a James Bond film, the Rinspeed sQuba is designed to run both on land and underwater. It can go down to 33 ft (10 m) in water and move like a submarine at a top speed of 2 mph (3 kph). Its open-top design means that passengers can escape easily in an emergency.

All about cars

ONCE UPON A TIME

• The first cars had **no steering wheels**: they were steered with a lever called a tiller.

• The first **accident** in a gas-powered car occurred in 1891, when the car swerved and crashed into a post. No one was hurt.

• The first **specially built car racetrack** was Brooklands in the UK, built in 1907.

• The first **car tires** were white.

• The 1904 Thomas Flyer, which had a removable hard top, is considered to be the first **convertible car**.

• The first **recorded speeding ticket** was issued in 1904 to Harry Myers, actor and director, for driving at 12 mph (19 kph).

• The first **electric traffic light**, with red and green signals, was invented in 1912 by American police officer Lester Wire. They were first installed on the streets of Cleveland, Ohio, in 1914.

ACCESSORIES

★ The **gas gauge** first appeared as a standard feature in 1922.

★ **License plates** were first issued in France in 1893 by the police.

★ **Airbags** were invented by John Hetrick, an industrial engineering technician, in 1951.

★ **Air conditioning** was introduced in 1939 by Nash Motors. This ventilation system was called the "Weather Eye."

★ A **rearview mirror** was first used in 1911 by Ray Harroun, a race car driver.

★ The first **car radio** was invented by the Galvin brothers, Paul and Joseph, in 1929.

★ **Electric windows** were first used in cars by the British car manufacturer Daimler in 1948.

★ The **windshield wiper** was invented by Mary Anderson in 1903.

★ The **three-point seatbelt**, which goes around the lap and over the shoulder, was first introduced in 1959 by Volvo.

★ A third **rear brake light**, mounted on the rear windshield, was invented in 1974 by US psychologist John Voevodsky.

KNOW YOUR CAR

♦ The **dashboard** was originally a piece of wood attached to the front of a horse-drawn carriage. It prevented mud from splattering the driver.

♦ **Flat, asphalt roads** were originally requested by cyclists, not drivers.

♦ The most **recycled product** in the world today is the car: about 95 percent of retired cars are recycled every year.

♦ **When idle**, a car uses 1.6 fl oz (0.05 liters) of gas in one minute.

♦ Toyota has said that an **average car is made up of** 30,000 parts and 3,000 ft (915 m) of electrical wire.

♦ Car manufacturers now place a small arrow next to the **fuel level icon** on the dashboard to show drivers which side of the car the fuel tank is on.

♦ An **out-of-range car remote** can be pressed 256 times before it stops working.

♦ If a car could be driven straight upward at 60 mph (100 kph), it would take about six months to **reach the Moon**.

♦ **One in four cars** are now manufactured in China.

♦ An **airbag inflates** within 40 milliseconds of a crash.

♦ Many cars can be driven for up to 60 miles (100 km) after the fuel tank is empty—this is called the **buffer zone**.

♦ Around **60 million cars** are produced each year—that's about 165,000 cars a day.

♦ Leonardo da Vinci made **drawings for a self-propelled vehicle** in the 1400s—at least 400 years before the car was invented.

Currently, more than 1 billion cars are in use around the world.

♦ On average, it takes **25 hours to build** a car, 10 of which are spent painting it.

♦ The **onboard computer** system in a standard modern car is more powerful than the ones that were used to send astronauts to the Moon in the 1960s and 1970s.

♦ If a car is **struck by lightning**, the passengers inside will usually be safe: the electricity is deflected around the car's metal frame.

RECORD BREAKERS

▶ The world's **heaviest limousine** is the *Midnight Rider*. It weighs more than 50,000 lb (22,680 kg) and has space for up to 40 people across a number of "rooms."

▶ The **least amount of time** taken to remove a car engine and replace it with a new one is 42 seconds. The car used was a Ford Escort.

▶ The world's **lowest street-legal car**—the *Flatmobile* built by Perry Watkins—is just 19 in (48 cm) high.

▶ The **longest limousine** is the 100-ft- (30.5-m-) long *American Dream*. It has 26 wheels and is hinged in the middle for turning corners.

▶ The **smallest roadworthy car** is the *Wind Up*, which measures 41 in (104 cm) high, 26 in (66 cm) wide, and 52 in (132 cm) long. It was built by Perry Watkins.

▶ The **longest jump by a monster truck** off a ramp is 237 ft 8 in (72.4 m). It was achieved by the American Joe Sylvester in his *Bad Habit* monster truck in 2013.

WONDERFUL CARS

★ The Volkswagen Beetle is the **best-selling car** of all time. A total of 21.5 million Beetles were sold from 1938 to 2003.

★ In 1916, **55 percent** of the world's cars were Ford Model Ts—a record that has never been beaten.

★ The **first car built** in the US was the Duryea, of which only one still exists today.

★ **More than 1 million** Chevrolet Impalas were sold in 1965, a record for a single year.

★ The world's **oldest running car**, a steam-powered model built in 1884 for Count De Dion in France, sold for $4.6 million in 2011.

★ The **Ford GT** is so strong that during its "roof crush" test it broke the machine.

★ The *Car-puccino* **runs on coffee**, converting used coffee grounds to flammable gas.

★ Volkswagen has **named several cars after winds**—"Passat," a German word for the trade winds; "Polo," after the polar winds; and "Bora," from the Bora winds.

The highest-ever speeding fine of $750,000 was paid in Switzerland. Fines there are based on speed and the driver's salary.

FORMULA 1

• While standard car engines can last for more than 10 years, F1 **car engines** last for only about two hours of racing.

• An F1 car **can accelerate** from 0–160 mph (0–258 kph) and decelerate back to zero within just four seconds.

• F1 **drivers** lose up to 9 lb (4 kg) of their body weight in just two hours of racing.

• The force an F1 driver feels when they **brake** their car is comparable to how it would feel to drive through a brick wall at a speed of 186 mph (300 kph).

• An F1 car is made up of **80,000 parts**.

• **Racing tires** last for only 56–75 miles (90–120 km), while standard car tires can last for 37,300–62,140 miles (60,000–100,000 km).

• The **tires** of most F1 cars are filled with nitrogen, as it has a more consistent pressure than normal air.

• An F1 driver **changes gears** 2,500–4,000 times during a race.

• **Pit stop crews** in F1 races take an average of three seconds to refuel and change tires.

AROUND THE WORLD

▶ One **Hong Kong** businessman recently placed an order for 30 Rolls-Royce cars, the single largest order for this car ever made.

▶ In **Japan**, drivers above 75 years of age have to mark the rear of their cars with the "Koreisha" symbol (elderly car mark).

▶ In **China**, you can pay to have someone drive your car through a traffic jam, while you are whisked away on a motorcycle.

▶ In **Albania**, 80 percent of registered cars are Mercedes-Benz.

▶ One of the longest recorded traffic jams, in **France** in 1980, stretched 110 miles (177 km).

▶ In the **US**, a driver spends an average of 38 hours a year waiting at red lights.

▶ The Kea, a bird native to **New Zealand**, is notorious for eating the strips of rubber from around car windows.

▶ In **Cyprus**, it is illegal to eat or drink anything while driving.

▶ In 1898, police in **New York City** used bicycles to pursue speeding drivers.

Glossary

Accelerate To speed up and go faster.

Aerodynamics The science of designing something to have a lower air resistance so it can move smoothly through the air. This makes it more efficient because it uses less energy and saves fuel.

Airbag A safety device usually packed in the center of the steering wheel and in the dashboard in front of the passenger seat. An airbag quickly inflates with air during a crash, cushioning a car's occupants from the impact.

Amphibious car A car that can operate on land and on water.

Axle The shaft (or rod) that car wheels turn on. The axle transmits power to the wheels and makes them turn.

Battery A store of chemicals that produce electricity when connected to a circuit.

Bumper A bar of metal, plastic, or rubber that is attached to the back and front of a car to protect it in the event of a collision.

cc (cubic centimeters) This is a measurement of the capacity, or space, inside all the cylinders of an engine. A larger cc usually means a more powerful engine.

Chassis The basic frame of a vehicle, upon which the engine and main body are mounted.

Clutch A device operated by a pedal that allows the driver to change gears. The clutch is operated by the driver's left foot.

Concept car A vehicle that is built to show new designs or technologies.

Convertible A car with a roof that can be folded back or removed.

Coupe A two-door car with a fixed roof that slopes down to the rear.

Crankshaft In an engine, the crankshaft is a rod that is turned by the power of the pistons pumping up and down. The crankshaft changes this up-and-down motion into a rotating motion that turns the car's wheels.

Crash test dummy A full-scale model of a person, used to test the safety of road vehicles in simulated collisions.

Crumple zone The area on a vehicle that absorbs force during a collision, helping to protect the occupants from injury.

Dashboard A panel inside the vehicle, below the windshield, that contains indicator dials (i.e., a speedometer), storage compartments, and controls.

Diesel A type of liquid fuel, made from oil. Diesel is used to power many trucks and some cars.

Disk brake A brake that reduces the speed of a car by using friction to slow down the wheels.

Drag racing A type of car race where two or more cars accelerate from a standing start and race for a fixed distance in a straight line.

Electric car A car with an engine powered solely by electricity.

Force A push or a pull action that can make things change direction, speed up, slow down, and even change shape.

Formula 1 (F1) A worldwide racing championship that uses extremely fast, single-seat racing cars built to strict rules (the "formula"). Races take place on tracks over many laps.

Four-stroke cycle The most common type of engine. Each piston in the engine works in four stages, or strokes: intake (taking in a mixture of air and gas), compression (squeezing the mixture), explosion (a spark ignites the mixture, which explodes and pushes the piston down), and exhaust (the spent mixture leaves the piston).

Four-wheel drive A system in which power from a vehicle's engine is sent to all four wheels.

Front-wheel drive A system in which power from a vehicle's engine is sent to the front wheels only.

Gasoline A liquid fuel used to power most of the cars on our roads. Gasoline is made from crude oil or gaseum, which is found deep under the Earth.

Gearbox The part of a vehicle that contains the gears.

Gears Toothed wheels that lock together. Gears are used to change the speed or force with which a car's wheels turn.

Gear stick A rod located by the driver's seat that is used in conjunction with the clutch to change gears.

Go-kart A small, low-slung motor vehicle with an exposed frame, often used for racing.

Grand tourer (GT) A high-performance, luxury car, able to make long journeys at high speeds in style and comfort.

Hatchback A car with a rear door that opens upward, revealing the trunk area.

Horsepower (hp) A unit of power. It is used to measure the power of a vehicle's engine. The term was invented more than 200 years ago to compare the amount of work a steam engine could do compared to a horse.

Hybrid A vehicle that uses two or more different power sources, such as gas and electricity.

Internal combustion engine An engine that burns fuel inside one or more cylinders, rather than in an exterior furnace. Most vehicles are powered by internal combustion engines.

Jet propelled car A car that is powered by a jet engine.

LED (light emitting diode) An LED is a small but bright light that is very energy efficient.

Limousine A long, luxury car, often with a partition that separates the driver from the passenger compartment.

Microcar The smallest type of car. A microcar has little internal space, a weak engine, and sometimes only three wheels.

Moose test A test that measures how well a car is able to avoid a sudden obstacle.

Minivan An minivan is a large vehicle able to carry up to eight passengers. They are also known as multipurpose vehicles.

Pickup truck A small truck with one bank of seats and a large, flat cargo area at the back.

Pit stop When a car leaves the track for repairs and refueling during a car race.

Production car A car that is mass-produced and sold to the general public.

Rallying A type of motorsport in which adapted production cars are driven over public roads or across rough terrain against a set time.

Roadster A sporty, open-topped car.

Running board A narrow platform attached to the sides of a vehicle that is used to climb in or out. Running boards were common on early cars, but are no longer used.

Sedan A four-door car for four or more people that has an enclosed trunk.

Solar car A car powered by the Sun's energy.

Speedometer A dial on the dashboard that shows the driver how fast the vehicle is moving.

Spoiler A small wing mounted on the back of a car to reduce lift at high speeds, which helps the car to grip the road better.

Standing start Some motorsports have a standing start, where cars are stationary at the beginning of the race.

Station wagon A car with an extended roofline. It has a floor to roof trunk space.

Steering wheel A wheel that the driver turns to change the direction of the front wheels. It is mounted on the dashboard.

Stock car racing A type of motorsport in which production cars are driven around an oval racetrack for a set number of laps.

Sunroof A panel in a car's roof that can be opened.

Supercar An expensive, high-performance car. Supercars have powerful engines.

Suspension A system of springs and shock absorbers that help a vehicle travel more smoothly over bumps in a road's surface.

SUV (sport utility vehicle) A rugged vehicle designed for off-road use, but often used on normal roads in urban areas.

Trunk A small, self-contained space, usually at the rear of a car, used for carrying goods such as luggage.

Turbocharged A turbocharged car is equipped with a turbocharger, which increases the engine's power.

VIN (vehicle identification number) A VIN is a unique code used to identify every individual vehicle.

Wind tunnel A large, tubelike passage with a huge fan at one end that is used to test the aerodynamics of cars and other objects.

Index

Acknowledgments

Dorling Kindersley would like to thank: Annabel Blackledge for proofreading; Helen Peters for indexing; and Fleur Star for editorial assistance.

The publishers would also like to thank the following for their kind permission to reproduce their photographs:

(Key: a-above; b-below/bottom; c-center; f-far; l-left; r-right; t-top)

1 Alamy Images: Tom Wood (c). 2-3 Dreamstime.com: Steve Allen (c). 4-5 Dreamstime.com: Leonello Calvetti (c). 5 Volvo Car Group: (br). 6 Alamy Images: Interfoto (tr); Motoring Picture Library (clb). Dreamstime.com: Hupeng (br). 7 Alamy Images: (cra, bc); Interfoto (c). Getty Images: Art Media / Print Collector (tl, tc). Rex Features: LAT Photographic (crb). 8 Alamy Images: Filmfoto-Akadit-tech (b). Getty Images: Oxford Science Archive / Print Collector (tl). TopFoto.co.uk: he Granger Collection, NYC (cra). 8-9 Getty Images: Fotosearch (b). 9 Alamy Images: Jim West (br). Getty Images: Car Culture (tl); Adeel Halim / Bloomberg (tr). 12-13 MINI Plant Oxford. 14-15 Reuters: Ints Kalnins (t). 15 Alamy Images: Colin Underhill (c). Dreamstime.com: Ensuper (br); Hansenn (tl); Goce Risteski (tr). Getty Images: Jeff Kowalsky / Bloomberg (cr). 16 Corbis: Louie Psihoyos (tl). 16-17 Corbis: Tim Wright (b). 17 123RF.com: Olexandr Moroz (tr). Alamy Images: Frank Herzog / culture-images GmbH (l). 20 Dreamstime.com: Lorenzo Dottorini. 21 Dreamstime.com: Dmitriy Melnikov (br). 22 Dorling Kindersley: National Motor Museum, Beaulieu (c). Courtesy Mercedes-Benz Cars, Daimler AG: (tl, tr). 22-23 Getty Images: Underwood Archives (t); Apic / Hulton Archive (b). 23 Dreamstime.com: Louie Petruzzi (ca). 25 Getty Images: SSPL (br). 26 Alamy Images: Carrumdrum (br). Dreamstime.com: (cla, c); James Steidl (bl). 27 Dorling Kindersley: (t). Giles Chapman Library: (b). 28-29 Alamy Images: KS_Autosport. 31 Alamy Images: National Motor Museum / Motoring Picture Library (b). 33 Alamy Images: Tom Wood (br). Jaguar Cars Limited: (t). 34 Volvo Car Group. 35 Dreamstime.com: Yocamon (br). 36 Dreamstime.com: Ddcoral (c). 36-37 Alamy Images: eVox / Drive Images (t). BMW Group: (b). 38 Dreamstime.com: Buschmen (br); Maxirf (cl); Teddyklung (bl). 39 Giles Chapman Library: (t). 40 Photoshot: Drive Images (b). Volvo Car Group: (t). 41 BMW Group: (c). 42 Getty Images: Yasbant Negi / India Today Group (br). Toyota (GB) PLC: (cl). 42-43 Audi AG: (t). 43 Courtesy Mercedes-Benz Cars, Daimler AG: (b). 46 Giles Chapman Library: (t). 45 Alamy Images: Motoring Picture Library (t). Giles Chapman Library: (b). 46 Alamy Images: Hans Dieter Seufert / culture-images GmbH (t); Motoring Picture Library (br). 47 Photoshot: Drive Images (t). 48 Alamy Images: National Motor Museum / Motoring Picture Library (br). 51 BMW Group: (t), (r). Photoshot: (b). 52 Corbis: Car Culture (t). Dreamstime.com:

Cheng Mao (b). 52-53 Alamy Images: nawson (t). 53 Alamy Images: P Cox (b). 54-55 Getty Images: Sean Gallup. 56 Audi AG: (tr). 56-57 BMW Group: (b). 57 Dreamstime.com: Stefan Ataman (t). 58 Alamy Images: B Christopher (cl). Dreamstime.com: Keith Bell (cla). Courtesy Mercedes-Benz Cars, Daimler AG: (tr). Photoshot: Gary Lee / UPPA (clb). 59 Alamy Images: National Motor Museum / Motoring Picture Library (b). Photoshot: Drive Images (t). 60 Dorling Kindersley: (b). 60-61 Courtesy Mercedes-Benz Cars, Daimler AG: (bc). 61 Audi AG: (t). Dreamstime.com: Stefan Ataman (br). 62 Corbis: Car Culture (b). Getty Images: Benjamin Auger / Paris Match (cr). 63 Alamy Images: Carlo Bollo (br). Giles Chapman Library: (t). 64 Courtesy Mercedes-Benz Cars, Daimler AG. 65 Alamy Images: National Motor Museum / Motoring Picture Library (t); Robert Steinbarth (b). 66 Dreamstime.com: Mile Atanasov (b). 66-67 Toyota (GB) PLC: (t). 67 Alamy Images: Marin Tomas (tr). 68-69 Rex Features: Snap Stills. 70 Lexus: (t). 71 Getty Images: Business Wire (b). Courtesy Mercedes-Benz Cars, Daimler AG: (tr). Photoshot: Drive Images (tl). Toyota (GB) PLC: (tc). 72 Corbis: Reuters (t). Courtesy Mercedes-Benz Cars, Daimler AG: (b). 73 Dreamstime.com: Keith Bell (br). Photoshot: Drive Images (t). 74 Audi AG: (cla). 74-75 BMW Group. 76 Rolls-Royce Motor Cars. 77 Rolls-Royce Motor Cars: (tl). 78-79 Rolls-Royce Motor Cars: (t). 79 Rolls-Royce Motor Cars: (tl). 79 BMW Group: (cra). iStockphoto.com: Tashatuvango (c). Rolls-Royce Motor Cars: (tl, c). 80-81 Dreamstime.com: Lucidwaters (t). 80 Volvo Car Group. 81 Alamy Images: Mark Bassett (b). 82-83 Press Association Images. 84 Alamy Images: National Motor Museum / Motoring Picture Library (b). 85 Corbis: Car Culture (t). 86 Dreamstime.com: Victor Torres (t). Photoshot: (bc). 86-87 Corbis: Car Culture (b). 88-89 Corbis: David Freers / Transstock (t). 88 Courtesy Mercedes-Benz Cars, Daimler AG: (br). 90 Getty Images: Michael Bradley / AFP (t). Getty Images: Saeed Khan / AFP (br). Pearson Asset Library: Coleman Yuen. Pearson Education Asia Ltd. (br/Background). 92 Getty Images: Nacho Cubero / AFP (b); Jonathan Ferrey (cr). 92-93 Alamy Images: Tony Watson (t). Getty Images: William West / AFP (b). 94 123RF.com: Gunter Nezhoda (clb). Daimler AG: (b). Dreamstime.com: Macleoddesigns (cra). 95 123RF.com: Fedor Selivanov (c). Corbis: Blaine Harrington III (crb). BMW Group: (bc). Pearson Asset Library: Coleman Yuen. Pearson Education Asia Ltd. (l/Background). 96 Corbis: Urbanandsport / Cordon Press (br). 97 Dreamstime.com: Bigknell (ca); Natpurports (bl). Getty Images: Paul Gilham (br). 98-99 Corbis: Leo Mason (b). 98 Getty Images: Rusty Jarrett (b). 99 Corbis: Juan DeLeon / Icon SMI (b). 100 Dreamstime.com: Bmaksym (t). Getty Images: John Harrelson (b). 101 Dreamstime.com: Christa Leigh Thomas (t). Getty Images: Darrell Ingham (b). 102 Alamy Images: Joe Fox Motorsport / Radharc Images (t). Corbis: Jo Lillini / Sport Concept Diffusion (b). 103 Alamy Images: pel / picturesbyrob. 104-105 Photoshot: Imago. 106 Getty Images: Rainer W. Schlegelmilch (b). 109 Audi AG: (b). 110 Alamy Images: Tom Wood (r). 111 Alamy Images: Phil

Talbot (b). Corbis: John Lamm / Transtock (tr). 112 Alamy Images: National Motor Museum / Motoring Picture Library (b). 112-113 Dreamstime.com: Hupeng. 113 Alamy Images: pbpgalleries (b). 114-115 Corbis: Bruce Benedict / Transtock. 116 Getty Images: David Taylor. 117 Getty Images: Alain Benainous / Gamma-Rapho (br). 118 Dreamstime.com: Max Herman (c). 118-119 Alamy Images: Bo Brown (b). 119 Carnegie Mellon University and NASA: (br). Corbis: Splash / WaterCar.com / / Splash News (b). Dreamstime.com: Olgavolodina (c). 120 Corbis: Sutton Images (bc). Photoshot: (cr). 121 Corbis: Owaki / Kulla (b). Dreamstime.com: Luchschen (bl); Danil Roudenko (t). 122 Alamy Images: eVox / Drive Images (t). Corbis: izmocars / Izmo (b). Dreamstime.com: Maxym622 (c). 122-123 Photoshot. 123 Alamy Images: Mark Eite / Afto Co. Ltd. (t). 124 Alamy Images: Motoring Picture Library (b). Corbis: Bettmann (tr). 125 Press Association Images: (b). Reuters: STR New (ca). 126 Alamy Images: Chuck Eckert (br); Johner Images (cl). Getty Images: Terry Moore / Stocktrek Images (bl). SuperStock: Tony Latham / Loop Images (cla). 127 Getty Images: Jim Watson / AFP (t). Rex Features: (b). 128 NASA: (b). 129 Corbis: NASA / JPL-Caltech. 130 Alamy Images: StockTrek / Purestock (b). 130-131 NASA. 132-133 Getty Images: Greg Wood / AFP. 134 Volvo Car Group. 135 Courtesy Mercedes-Benz Cars, Daimler AG: (t, b). 136 Used with permission, GM Media Archives: (t). Volvo Car Group: (b). 136-137 Courtesy Mercedes-Benz Cars, Daimler AG: (t). 137 Jaguar Cars Limited: (ca). 138 Dreamstime.com: Patrick Poendl (t). Jaguar Cars Limited: (b). 139 Audi AG. 140 Getty Images: Kimimasa Mayama / Bloomberg (t). Toyota (GB) PLC: (b). 141 Audi AG: (t). Toyota (GB) PLC: (b). 142 Alamy Images: Phil Talpin (t). Dreamstime.com: Kevin M. Mccarthy (b). 143 Dreamstime.com: Red (t). Photoshot: (br); Xinhua (b). 144-145 Rinspeed Inc.

Jacket images: Front: 123RF.com: Fedor Selivanov bl, cr (Porsche 918 Spyder RSR); Audi AG: cla/ (Audi TT RS Roadster), bc/ (Audi TT alt); Daimler AG: cb/ (F1 W05); Alamy Images: Anthony Pozner Hendon Way Motors c, Gilbert and Anna East cb, National Motor Museum, Beaulieu cr/ (Steam-powered Cugnot), Tata Motors br; BMW Group: cb/ (BMW 530d Gran Turismo), cb/ (BMW 335i), cra/ (BMW 3 Series Convertible), ca/ (Rolls-Royce Phantom Coupe), cl; Jaguar Cars Limited: cra, cra/ (Jaguar XJ), bl/ (Jaguar C-X16); Lexus: bc; Courtesy Mercedes-Benz Cars, Daimler AG: cb/ (Mercedes-Benz F700), ca/ (Motorized carriage), cr, cla, cra/ (Mercedes-Benz F700); Toyota (GB) PLC: cb/ (Toyota RAV4), bc/ (Toyota i-Road), ca; Volvo Car Group: crb; Back: Audi AG: cr; Dorling Kindersley: Tata Motors cla; Courtesy Mercedes-Benz Cars, Daimler AG: cla/ (Mercedes-Benz GL Class); Spine: Dorling Kindersley: Anthony Pozner Hendon Way Motors t

All other images © Dorling Kindersley

For further information see:
www.dkimages.com